DR

DROITWICH

Please return/renew this item by the last date shown

worcestershire
countycouncil
Libraries & Learning

THE SUNDAY TIMES

Successful Time Management

Patrick Forsyth | Revised Second Edition

LONDON   PHILADELPHIA   NEW DELHI

Publisher's note
Every possible effort has been made to ensure that the information contained in this book is accurate at the time of going to press, and the publishers and author cannot accept responsibility for any errors or omissions, however caused. No responsibility for loss or damage occasioned to any person acting, or refraining from action, as a result of the material in this publication can be accepted by the editor, the publisher or the author.

First published 2003
Second edition 2007
Reprinted 2007
Revised second edition 2010

120 Pentonville Road	525 South 4th Street, #241	4737/23 Ansari Road
London N1 9JN	Philadelphia PA 19147	Daryaganj
United Kingdom	USA	New Delhi 110002
www.koganpage.com		India

ISBN   978 0 7494 5550 7
E-ISBN   978 0 7494 5918 5

The views expressed in this book are those of the author, and are not necessarily the same as those of Times Newspapers Ltd.

British Library Cataloguing-in-Publication Data

A CIP record for this book is available from the British Library.

Library of Congress Cataloging-in-Publication Data

Forsyth, Patrick.
    Successful time management / Patrick Forsyth. -- Rev. 2nd ed.
      p. cm.
    ISBN 978-0-7494-5550-7
    1. Time management. I. Title.
    HD69.T54F678 2010
    650.1'1--dc22

                             2009038495

Typeset by Jean Cussons Typesetting, Diss, Norfolk
Printed and bound in India by Replika Press Pvt Ltd

Contents

Note to the revised edition

Any author is pleased if a book continues in print for a while, but in this case it is perhaps no surprise to find this title due to reprint and appear in a revised form. Time management is a perennial issue, one where good practice can enhance the performance and success of almost any executive or manager, in any business and at any level.

The main lessons here all remain relevant. Indeed the necessity for effective time management has, if anything, been heightened by the economic conditions of recent months, which have set changes in train that look like having implications for quite a while yet; hence the inclusion of a short appendix (Appendix 1) addressing this situation. Beyond that changes are more minor, though sufficient to ensure the book still provides a state of the art statement of best time management practice.

Any writer of how-to material would like to think that what they write can be useful. Certainly this is my belief regarding this topic; and, given the subject matter, it is not exaggerating to say that there are ideas here that can change your life, rapidly allowing improved personal and corporate performance and greater effectiveness as you manage to do more and concentrate more accurately on key issues.

That said – do read on: you have nothing to lose but some bad or inappropriate habits.

Preface

The day is of infinite length for him
who knows how to appreciate and use it

Goethe

If you are busy then you are normal. The modern workplace is unrelenting and deadlines, pressure (and, if you let it get to you, stress too) and a daily avalanche of e-mails are the order of the day. Dealing with this must be part of everyone's stock in trade. The fact that this book is being produced in a second edition is a sign of the perennial nature of its subject.

You are doubtless judged by what you do, by the results you achieve. To survive and prosper you have to be productive, efficient and effective. Time management is about working actively to create efficiency and effectiveness in a way that makes achieving your targeted results more likely. Success does not just happen. You make it happen. So too with your work pattern: *you* create it and do so for good or ill. Here we examine an essential foundation to success.

Good, effective time management is a core skill, a career skill that we all need both to make us able to perform in a current job

and to enhance our career prospects. It is a real differentiating
factor, one where getting to grips with it can see you consistently
achieving what you want in both job and career in a way that
gives you an edge on other people, perhaps of equal ability, but
who lack this aspect of self-organisation and discipline.
Addressing this area is not in any sense an option. It is not that
being an effective time manager would be somehow 'nice' or
maybe 'useful'; it is essential to making your work and career
successful.

Making a difference

The overall principles of time management are straightforward. It
has been said that you should: *do what's important, and ignore
what isn't* and that *urgent things are only important things that were
not addressed when they originated.* True enough, but
oversimplifying does not make tackling the details any easier.
The process needs application and commitment if some of the
elements of good time management are to be put into practice. As
things become engrained as habit it becomes easier. But
becoming, and remaining, well organised *is* possible. It is not
rocket science; indeed what needs to be done is largely common
sense. But it is a matter of getting the details right – there is no
magic formula, and there are many factors to consider. This book
reviews the key approaches, and sets out the techniques and a
whole raft of tips to make you more productive. It is designed to
be practical, and to make implementation manageable.

Reviewing the process is the first step to improving what you
do with your time. You can make a difference, and you will like
the difference you make. If you work smarter (rather than just
longer and harder), then you will achieve more and find your job
less stressful and more satisfying.

Of course, you must read the book and that takes a while
(though by definition a good book about time management is
surely a short one, as this is). Consider it an investment – take a

little time now and you can save a significant amount of time every day thereafter. If you can certainly use some extra time, then that again shows that you are normal.

1

Time: a key resource – opportunities and difficulties

Success is a process, a quality of mind and way of being, an outgoing affirmation of life.

Alex Noble

Whatever job you do, if you are in a management or executive role, you will utilise a number of resources. People, money, materials – all are important. In any particular job, one resource may predominate. But there is one resource we all have in common: time. And time is a hard taskmaster. Everyone occasionally experiences problems getting everything done, and doing it all in the time available. For some, such problems seem perpetually to exist to one degree or another; others will admit to having moments when things seem to conspire to prevent work going as planned, and a few to living in a state of permanent chaos.

Who then needs to think about time management? Everyone, potentially, can benefit from reviewing how to manage their time effectively. In any organisation many of the things that actually characterise its very nature make proper time management difficult: hierarchical structures, people, deadlines, paperwork, e-mail, computer problems, meetings, pressures and interactions, both around the organisation and externally; all these and more can compound the problems.

This book aims to help solve the problems of time management for all those working in executive or managerial positions within organisations, whether commercial or otherwise, and who are charged with getting things done and achieving results. If you are in this category, even if you have already made strenuous attempts to organise the way you work, then you may pick up ideas that will help you achieve more. If you see yourself as having too much to do, if you have too little time in which to do it, if coping with the urgent means you never get to all the important things on your list, and you would like to be more organised and do not quite know how to go about becoming so, then this book is directed at you. If your desk is piled with untidy heaps of paper, you are constantly subject to interruptions, your deadlines are impossible and you despair of ever being able to get your head above water, then this book is definitely for you.

Time management is not optional. It is something that everyone who wants to work effectively must consider, whether formally or informally. In fact, virtually everyone practises time management to some degree; the only question is how well they do it and how it affects what they do. Yet, time management is not easy – as you may have noticed! Nor, even for those who work at it, is it something that anyone gets 100 per cent right. If you think that is a rather ominous start to a book on time management, there is worse to come. The classic author G K Chesterton wrote: 'The Christian ideal has not been tried and found wanting. It has been found difficult; and left untried.' So too with time management: just because it is difficult, the temptation can be to despair of ever making a real difference, and to give up on it, letting things take their course and muddling through somehow. To varying degrees, this temptation is often very strong.

Making it work

But, and it is a positive but, you can make a difference and such a difference cannot only be worthwhile, it can have a radical effect on both job and career. Make no mistake: the effect of getting to grips with time management can be considerable and varied. It can:

- **Affect your efficiency, effectiveness and productivity. This alone makes your attitude to time management very important, for it affects your work day by day, hour by hour, all the time.**
- **Condition the pressure that goes with any job.**
- **Create greater positive visibility. Time management is something that will influence how you are perceived by others within the organisation. Good time management is an overriding factor that can differentiate people of otherwise equal talent and ability, making it more likely that some will succeed better in career terms than others.**

Thus, although it may take some time, getting to grips with your own personal system of time management is immensely important. Time management must be seen as synonymous with self-management; it demands discipline, but discipline reinforced by habit. In other words, the good news is that it gets easier as you work at it. Good habits help ensure a well-organised approach to the way you plan and execute your work. On the other hand, bad habits – as many of us are aware – are difficult to shift. And the changing of habits is something that may well be a necessary result of any review of how you work.

Making time management work for you is based on two key factors: how you plan your time and how you implement the detail of what you do. The first of these, which is reviewed in the early part of this book, creates an important foundation upon which you can then build and work. The second consists of a multitude of operational factors, practices, methods and tricks, all of which can individually and positively affect the way in which you work. Such factors may be absurdly simple, for example, visibly checking your watch from time to time will tend to make visitors less likely to overstay their welcome, especially if such checks are accompanied by the appropriate look of concern. Or they may demand more complexity, for example, a well-set-up filing system can save time, ensuring that you can locate papers quickly and accurately.

Other factors may be downright sneaky, like having a private signal to prompt your secretary to interrupt a meeting with news of something demanding its rapid curtailment or your prompt departure. Furthermore, there is a cumulative effect at work here. This means that the more you adopt or adapt the tricks of the trade that work for you, the more time-efficient you become. This is a process that most of us can continue to add to and work on throughout our career. So, unless you are a paragon of time-efficient virtue, a review of whether you are working in the best possible way is nearly always worthwhile. Indeed, it can pay dividends to keep a regular eye on this throughout your working life. This too can become a habit.

A personal approach

Because of the way time management works, influenced as it is by many things, what works in any particular kind of job or for any particular individual will vary. Some of the ideas you will find presented here, or elsewhere, you will be able to add profitably to your own working habits. Some will be new to you; some you will know but may not be utilising as effectively as you might. Others will be able to form only the basis of what will suit you. They will need personalising, tailoring to the circumstances in which you work, and it is always important to consider this option with any idea you review before rejecting it.

Be careful not to reject out of hand anything that might be

useful in amended form. This is an area where every small influence can assist your overall productivity. Of course, some ideas will not suit you at all. However much you tinker with them, they will not form a useful basis for the kind of way in which you work. So be it. The aim should be to review thoroughly and then use every possible way to enhance the productivity of your job. What matters is arriving at a point where you are content that, having explored the possibilities for action, you have selected, adapted and experimented with all the methods that can realistically fit in with the way you work and assist your productivity. It is you who matters ultimately, not the principles. However, do remember that anything – but anything – that can help should be considered and, unless it has a negative impact, made part of your working practice. Good time management comes from leaving no stone unturned.

The productivity gain

Time may be relative, but it is a resource as valuable as any other. Yet, it is so easy to squander. Why is it that the thought and effort given to the appropriate use of other resources, money for instance, is so much greater than for time? The sheer difficulty of some aspects of time management and the power of habit explain some of this, but there is, I think, another reason.

Long ago Peter Cook appeared in a sketch about the possibility of a nuclear war, when it was said that the early warning radar would give four minutes' warning of any enemy missiles aimed our way. 'What can you do in four minutes?', asked one character incredulously. 'Some people', came the reply, 'can run a mile in four minutes!' Though sadly inadequate for the task of escaping from annihilation, four minutes is still, well, four minutes, and it is an important principle of time management that even small periods of time can readily add up to a worthwhile amount.

Consider four minutes saved – by not running that mile

perhaps. It is easy to think of it as not worthwhile. However, if the four minutes is saved by increasing efficiency on one small task undertaken regularly, then for something done every day that adds up to more than 14 hours over a year! That is very nearly as much as two working days, and should give anyone pause for thought. What could you do – extra – with two additional working days? It is undeniably a useful amount of time and most people have probably got a dozen jobs on their list that could be got out of the way if an additional two days were really available. This thought comes from imagining what speeding up just one small regular task or perhaps avoiding wasting time, to the tune of just four minutes, could do for you. So, another significant reason why time management may be neglected is that individual small savings of time may seem unimportant. We tend to wonder what five minutes here or there matters, when what is really needed is a clear hour or day without interruptions. Yet, clearly, such short moments add up.

If this fact is recognised, and time and activities planned accordingly, then it is possible to free up considerable amounts of time. What is more, this can often be done at minimal cost. This is worth noting, as many potential improvements to efficiency do have a cost. If you want new equipment, more in your budget, or additional people, then in many organisations this needs considerable justification and may still be turned down. But your time is yours to utilise. It is an area where you can make a real difference to performance armed with little more than the intention to do so.

Speculate to accumulate

A further point needs stating before we turn to areas of individual action. You will find that some ways of saving time, or utilising it better, do need an investment – but it is an investment of time. It may seem like a contradiction in terms, having to spend time to save time. Again, this can all too easily become a barrier to action.

Yet the principle is clear: there is a time equation that can and must be put to work if time is to be brought under control. There are many ways of ensuring that time is utilised to best effect, and, while some take only a moment, others take time either to set up or for you to adopt the habit of working in a particular way.

Consider an example, one linked to delegation, a subject we return to later, and to the commonly heard phrase 'It's quicker to do it myself.' When this thought comes to mind, sometimes, and certainly in the short term, the sentiment may well be correct. It is quicker to do it yourself. But beware, because this may only be true at the moment something occurs. Say someone telephones you requesting certain information, imagine also that you must locate and look something up, compose a brief explanatory note and send the information off to the other person. It is a minor matter and will take you three or four minutes. Imagine further that, to avoid the task, you consider letting your secretary do it. Explaining and showing him or her what needs to be done will certainly take 10–15 minutes of your time and your secretary's. It really is quicker to do it yourself. Not so, certainly not if it is a regularly occurring task. If it happens 10 times a week, say, then if you take time to brief your secretary he or she will only have to take it on for less than a week and the time spent briefing will have paid off. Thereafter you save a significant amount of time every week, indeed on every occasion that similar requests are made in the future. This is surely worthwhile. The time equation here of time spent as a ratio of time saved works positively. This is often the case, and allows worthwhile savings to be made, both to simple examples and to more complex matters where hours or days spent on, say, reorganising a system or process may still pay dividends.

So, why is it so difficult to take this sort of action? Why is the world full of people saying that it is quicker to do some things themselves? Some of the reasons may be to do with attitudes to delegation (of which more later); beyond that it is largely habit and lack of thought – and perhaps the pressure of the moment. We judge that it is possible to pause for the few moments necessary to get another task out of the way, but somehow not for long enough to carry out a briefing that would rid us of the task altogether, and ultimately make a real time saving. It is worth a thought. Become determined not to be caught in this time trap and you are en route to saving a great deal of time.

Given the right intention, and motivation, it is possible for anyone to improve their time utilisation, and to do so markedly if you have not thought about it recently. Make no mistake, however, the process does not stop there. It takes more than a review of time management and the adoption of one or two ideas to make you truly productive for life. A review can kick-start the process, but the right way of thinking must continue it. The best time managers have not only instilled in themselves good habits and so put part of the process on auto pilot, so to speak, they also view time management as an area of perpetual fine-tuning. In everything they do the time dimension is considered. It becomes a prerequisite for the various ways in which they work. And they continuously strive to improve still further – changing the way they work and what it allows them to achieve. That fine-tuning too becomes a habit.

Perfect time

One final introductory point. Time management is very much an area where the old saying 'Never let perfection be the enemy of the good' is entirely appropriate. However well you approach the management of your time, you are never going to be able to regard it as perfect. Nothing will guarantee that you will never be unable to find anything again, nor will it mean nothing takes longer in future than you think it will, nor that you are never interrupted again, not least at a crucial moment. Remember Murphy's Law: that if something can go wrong or turn out inconveniently it will. Nor does it mean that you will never again find yourself saying: 'If only I had more time...'. Indeed, in many jobs there is a creative element. You are employed to make things happen, to innovate, review and change things and to do so in a dynamic environment where it sometimes seems that nothing stays the same for five whole minutes. It is inherent in such circumstances that there will always be new things to do and that, as a consequence, you will never get to the bottom of the 'Things to do' list. The time to worry is not when you have too much to do, but more when you do not have enough to do.

But though perfection may not be possible, improvement certainly is. Every saving of time, every productivity gain, whether large or small, adds to the total way in which your style of working contributes to your effectiveness. Any aspect of a job can probably be changed for the better, in terms of how it is done, to use time more productively. This means that you must actively organise what you do and how you do it to produce optimum working and to be really effective. It is this process that using the principles of time management and adopting the right attitude can assist. Doing this and doing it thoroughly will benefit you and your organisation; and some of those benefits can come quickly.

Note: Corporate culture is becoming increasingly aggressive in its focus on productivity in the sense of hours worked. More and more people are spending more and more hours on the job, willingly or not. Yet there is plenty of evidence which states that extra hours do not translate directly into increased productivity, not least because stress and tiredness dilute effectiveness.

It is difficult for an individual to challenge this culture, but it should not be followed slavishly. The ideas of effective time management operate within some definition of the 'working day', and that will vary for every individual. Just simply adding hours unthinkingly can only achieve so much. The intention here is to show that changing habits and enhancing effectiveness by adopting the right way of working pay dividends. If you do this and achieve your objectives, then maybe the pressure to just 'put in more time' will decrease. If you are managing other people and creating the culture then this aspect may be worth a moment's thought (and you could do worse than to read my book *How to Motivate People*, also published by Kogan Page).

2

First steps towards effective time management

Tomorrow is always the busiest day of the week.

Jonathon Lazear

There are many activities where the whole is greater than the sum of the individual parts. For instance, juggling with flaming torches necessitates more than specific movements of the hands. Avoiding burning holes in the carpet depends also on overall coordination, concentration and getting the individual movements exactly right. Time management is similar. The individual techniques, ideas and tricks of the trade will allow you to make some progress towards an effective and efficient way of working, but only approaching the process on a broad front will lead to sustained practice that will ensure continuing effectiveness. Unless the right attitude is adopted, then time management will never be more than an initial enthusiastic embracing of techniques, which are then allowed rapidly to atrophy.

Thus, time management involves not just keeping your paperwork tidy and your desk clear, but a whole way of working that underlies all your actions and interfaces with all facets of your job. Because of this we review next a number of all-embracing rather than individual factors that need to be applied with an eye on the whole of the rest of your job and the range of tasks it entails. They start, logically enough, with the need to assess how you work now as a basis for considering action and possibly changes in the future.

Your work mix

Whatever your individual job, whether you are manager or executive, and regardless of the type of organisation for which you work and the functional area in which you are involved, you doubtless have many different things to do; too many perhaps. These are different in nature and complexity, and involve different timescales. They range across 1,001 things, from drafting a letter or report to planning the relocation of the entire organisation to new offices or the launching of a new product. What is more, you probably have a good many things on the go at once as well as overlapping, perhaps conflicting, priorities. Often work feels just like the juggling example on the previous page, and your 'reach' – how much you can keep on the go at once – is an important aspect of your effectiveness. If you exceed your reach then, like the juggler, the danger is that you do not simply drop one torch but several. It helps, when considering managing all of this effectively, to categorise the many elements. There are doubtless many ways of doing this, but just four categories seem to bring some order to the picture:

1. **Planning.** This is the prerequisite to all action. Many tasks are involved: research, investigation, analysis and testing amongst others. This area may also involve consultation and ultimately the communication of plans and is, of course, the key to decision making.
2. **Implementation.** Simply stated, doing things – of all sorts – whether intangible (of which the key one is making

decisions) or tangible. Specific tasks divide into two sorts. First, individual tasks. These are free-standing. They may be major or minor. For example, a writing task may entail composing a two-line e-mail or a 20-page report. Second, progressing tasks where a series of closely linked actions contribute cumulatively to achieving an overall result. Moving offices would involve such actions and such things may be more clearly visualised rather than described – indeed flowcharts provide a useful and time-efficient way of working on them. Tasks in both categories may well need to be linked to planning activity on whatever scale.

3. **Monitoring and control.** Checking may well be necessary to ensure things are being done in the best possible way and bringing the desired results. Checking may be simple, editing the draft of a report or running it through the spellchecker, for example. Or it may be complex, as are many financial control systems.

4. **Communicating and dealing with people.** This clearly overlaps with the other three categories of activity, but is inherent in the work of almost everyone. Few, if any, people work in isolation from others, and for most, the people issues, whether it is briefing them or reporting to them, meetings and other forms of communication with them, are an essential part of their work and take up a major part of their time.

In all four categories, there will or should be a strong link with objectives and achievement of results. All tasks and all actions should focus on the overall aims and are often of little significance in themselves. Effectiveness is measured ultimately by achievement. Time management must not be seen as only concerned with packing more activity into the available time, though this may be part of it; it must be instrumental in ensuring that objectives are met. It may be a cliché, but it must not be forgotten that activity must never be confused with achievement. With this picture in mind, we can look specifically at current working practice.

Assessing your current working practice

You may think that you know how you work; perhaps you feel you know all too well – warts and all. But do not be misled into thinking that considering in detail how you do things is a waste of time. Classically, improving anything implies the identification of how it is now. This gives a measure against which to judge how we might progress. Further, such an analysis can provide valuable information about where the greatest improvement may be found, all of which makes improvement more likely. This is certainly true of time management, more so perhaps because this is an area where there is a real tendency to self-delusion. If I ask if you spend too much time in meetings, you may well agree. But do you waste time doing unnecessary paperwork or do you socialise too much? Are you badly organised? Such questions are more likely to put us on the defensive, and understandably so. You are no doubt essentially efficient, but improvement may still be possible. Indeed, most people would value more time to complete their tasks and undertake their responsibilities, if this were possible. For most, it is.

To make other than superficial changes, you need to know something about your own working practices and pressures, and where time goes at present. In a complex job, many activities are involved.

Where time goes now

There are two ways to consider this. The first is to estimate it, guesstimate if necessary. This is most easily done in percentage terms on a pie chart (see Figure 2.1).

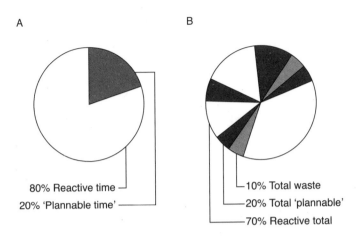

Figure 2.1   Planning limited 'plannable time'

The second is to use a time log (see Figure 2.2) to obtain a much more accurate picture – literally recording what you do through the day and doing so for at least a week, longer if you can (the chore of noting things down takes only a few seconds, but must be done punctiliously).

Few people keep a log without surprising themselves, and the surprises can be either that much more time is spent in some areas than you think, or that certain things take up less time than you think – mainly the former. Some obvious areas for review usually come to mind as a result.

Again using the simple pie chart, it can be useful as a second stage of this review to list what you would ideally like the time breakdown to be. This puts a clear picture in your mind of what you are working towards. Such a picture might even be worth setting out before you read on.

All this gives you something to aim towards and will tell you progressively – as you take action – whether that action is having a positive effect. If all the remaining review points are looked at

No.	Start time	Activity description	Time taken (minutes)	Priority* category A B C D	Comments
1					
2					
3					
4					
5					
6					
7					
8					
9					
10					
11					
12					
13					
14					
15					
16					
17					
18					
19					
20					
21					
22					
23					

Name: _____   Comments: _____

Date:

*Link these columns to any priority code you use   Total time taken (minutes): _____

Figure 2.2   Personal time performance log (example)

alongside this information then you can see more clearly whether you are able to take action to improve things, and whether the points refer to areas that are critical for you. With all this in mind, we turn to what is both one of the basics of time management and perhaps its most practically important tenet.

Plan the work and work the plan

Certainly any real progress with time management needs a plan. This must be in writing and must be reviewed and updated regularly; for most people this means a daily check. I repeat: a written plan and a regular check and update. It is thus what is sometimes called a rolling plan. Not only is it updated regularly, it provides a snapshot of your workload ahead at any particular moment. As such it should show accurately and completely your work plan for the immediate future, and give an idea of what lies beyond. As you look ahead there will be some things that are clear, for example when an annual budget must be prepared and submitted. Other areas are less clear and, of course, much cannot be anticipated at all in advance. At its simplest, such a plan is just a list of things to do. It may include:

- a daily plan;
- a weekly plan;
- commitments that occur regularly (weekly or monthly or annually);
- a plan for the coming month (perhaps linked to a planning chart).

The exact configuration will depend on the time span across which you work. What is important is that it works for you, that it is clear, that different kinds of activity show up for what they are and that it links clearly to your diary and appointment system. How such a list is arranged and how you can use it to improve your work and effectiveness are important, but the fact of the system and the thinking that its regular review prompts are also important in their own right. It is the basic factor in creating a time management discipline, and it provides much of the information from which you must make choices – what you do, delegate, delay or ignore, in what order you tackle things and so on. Good time management does not remove the need to make decisions of this sort, but it should make them easier and quicker to make and it should enable you to make decisions that really do help in a positive way, so that you get more done and in the best way to achieve your aims.

If this is already beginning to sound like hard work, do not despair. I do not believe that the process of updating and monitoring your rolling plan will itself become an onerous task. It will vary a little day by day, and is affected by your work pattern, but on average it is likely to take only a few minutes. I reckon I keep a good many balls in the air and am a busy person. My own paperwork on this takes perhaps five minutes a day, but – importantly – this prevents more time being taken up in less organised juggling during the day.

Dealing with the uncontrollable

A final point here is crucial. Some people, perhaps most, have a measure of their day that is reactive. Things occur that cannot be predicted, at least individually, and a proportion of the available time is always going to go in this way. Such activity is not automatically unimportant, and the reverse may well be true. For example, a manager on the sales or marketing side of a commercial company may have enquiries and queries coming from customers that are very important and must be dealt with promptly, but will nevertheless make fitting in everything else more difficult. Sometimes the reaction to this is to believe that, because of this reactive element, it is not possible to plan or to plan effectively. The reverse is true. If your days do consist, even in part, of this sort of random activity, it is even more important to plan because there is inherently less time available to do the other things that the job involves and that time has to be planned even more thoroughly to maximise its effectiveness.

Everyone needs a plan and everyone can benefit from having a clear view of what there is to be done. If you do not have this then the work of setting it up will take a moment, but it is worthwhile and it need not then take long to keep up to date. Once it is in place, you can evolve a system that suits you and that keeps up with the way in which your job and its responsibilities change over time.

What kind of system?

So far I have ignored the question of what paperwork is needed for this planning process. Many books on the subject of time management are closely linked to some specific proprietary time management system, consisting of diaries, files, binders and so on. Some even claim that the only route to time efficiency lies with their particular system. Now this may be fine if the system suits you, but I would suggest caution before taking up any particular one.

I will recommend no one system; I do not in fact use a branded system myself. This is not to say that I disapprove of them. One highly organised person I know uses one and swears by it, but I also know people who are the very opposite of organised and yet whose desks are adorned with the binders and card indices of their chosen system, so they certainly offer no kind of panacea. Many are restrictive, that is, they can only be used in a particular way and that may well not suit you and the way you think and work. There is thus a real danger that if you use a system and some element of it does not work for you, then your use of the whole system falters. A better way is perhaps to work out what you need first, asking:

- **What kind of diary do I need?**
- **How much space do I need for notes?**

- **How many sections fit the way my tasks are grouped?**
- **What permanent filing is necessary? etc.**

Then, when you have thought through what you need and worked that way for a while (a process that will almost certainly have you making a few changes in the light of how things actually work), you can check out the systems and see whether any of them formalise what you want to do and, as they can be expensive, make the investment worthwhile. Otherwise, many people organise themselves perfectly well with no more than a diary, a notebook or a file. To end with something of a recommendation, I would suggest that a loose-leaf diary system is a good basis for many (I use a desk-sized Filofax). This combines a neat system with the flexibility to include exactly what you need, and that is what is most important. After all, it must reflect your plan and it is your time that you want to organise. Of course, another option these days is to go electronic, so any form may be on screen rather than paper; but the same thinking applies to selecting what is best.

Realism suggests that no one system is right for everyone. Even the precise kind of diary layout you choose must be a personal decision based on your needs, and what else is necessary will reflect the way you work. You must decide for yourself; I can only state that all my experience suggests that a flexible and thus tailor-made system is likely to be best.

Setting clear objectives

Any plan is only as good as the objectives that lie behind it. Clear objectives (the text below defines these) really are important, and any lack of clarity can affect every aspect of a person's work, not least time management, sometimes doing so surreptitiously.

SMART objectives

Maxims advocating setting clear objectives are everywhere; they offer sound advice. You do need clear objectives, and they must not be vague or general hopes. A much quoted acronym spells out the principles involved: objectives should be SMART, that is: Specific, Measurable, Achievable, Realistic, and Timed. An example will help make this clear. A perennial area of management skill, on which I regularly conduct training, is that body of skills necessary for making formal presentations. Incidentally, any weakness in this area will waste time, tending to result in longer, and perhaps more agonising, preparation. Good presentation skills save time. But I digress.

It is all too easy to define the objectives for a workshop on this topic as being simply to ensure participants 'make better presentations', a statement that is unlikely to be sufficiently clear to be really useful. Objectives for a presentation skills course should be:

- *Specific.* To enable participants to make future presentations in a manner and style that will be seen as appropriate by their respective audiences, and which will enhance the message they put over.
- *Measurable.* In other words, how will we know this has been achieved? Ultimately, in this case, by the results of future presentations; but we might also consider that the trainer or the group, or both, will be able to judge this to a degree at the end of the event by observing the standard during practice.
- *Achievable.* Can this be done? The answer in this case will depend on the prevailing standard before the course. If the people are inexperienced and their standard of presentation is low, then the answer may be that it cannot. If, as we assume for the sake of our

developing example, they are people who are
sufficiently senior, experienced and with some practice
in the area of presentations, then the objectives should
be achievable – given a suitable amount of time and a
suitable programme.
- *Realistic.* Picking up the last point, if the time is, say,
inadequate then the objectives may not be realistic.
Potentially, these people can be improved, we might say,
but not in one short session.
- *Timed.* In training terms, this will reflect the timing of
the course. It may be scheduled to take place in one
month's time, so the objectives cannot be realised
before then. Also consider the duration: is a one, two or
any other number of days' programme going to do the
job?

Much of what needs to be done to manage time effectively is
concerned with tackling conflicts and making decisions about
what comes first, and none of this is possible if there is no
underlying clarity about objectives to act as a reference.

This is not the place for a long treatise on objective setting.
Suffice it to say that this is important to everything in corporate
life. A company functions best with clear corporate objectives,
the management structure works best when individuals are clear
about what it is they are expected to achieve. Consider your own
position. Are there any areas that are not clear in this respect? Do
objectives make for problems or conflict regarding the way you
go about the job? If you answered 'yes' to the first question, then
you probably did the same for the second. *Note:* you will never be
a good time manager unless you have clear objectives as part of
your overall job description. If you do not, this is something you
must seek to resolve.

At this point, we can take stock of some of the key issues on
the table. If you have an idea of where time goes now and how
you really approach things, if you have a (written) plan – relating
clearly to your job objectives – then you can get to work with
some hopes of being reasonably productive. But there are many

factors that can work to increase that productivity. Some are not only fundamental, but are also good examples of the way in which approaches (ultimately habits) can exert a considerable and ongoing influence on your working practices. The examples that follow are all potentially of great value to the manager wanting to become truly time-efficient.

Thinking ahead

This might appropriately be called the opposite of the 'if only...' school of ineffective time management. Too often people find themselves in a crisis, the resolution of which would be all too easy if we could wind the clocks back. 'If only we had done so and so earlier...' we say as we contemplate a messy and time-consuming process of unscrambling. In all honesty, though the unexpected can happen sometimes, crisis management is all too common, and often all too unnecessary. Coping well with crises saves time – certainly if the alternative is panic. The text below and on the following page makes some comments on coping with crisis.

Don't panic

Whatever the cause and implications of any crisis situation, the rule has to be 'Never treat a crisis like a crisis.' Panic implies an absence of all the usual management processes that are no less needed at such a time; perhaps they are needed in fuller measure than usual. Having a systematic approach in mind (and acquiring the habit of referring to it, albeit mentally) as a first conscious step to avoiding panic is useful. Blind, unthinking action will rarely have the precision required to rescue the situation and more damage may be done – and more time wasted – as further second-stage action becomes necessary. So, the rules are:

- Stay cool and do not panic.
- Think (and what is more, take sufficient time to think straight).
- Consider the full range of management skills that could sort out the situation (this may include simple tactics such as delegating certain straightforward actions to give you time to resolve more complex issues, and more radical solutions, such as reviewing policy).
- Make an action plan (especially important if there is any degree of complexity involved).
- Consider the control aspect of that ongoing action plan (simplistically creating a mechanism to show progress and let you know when the crisis is past).

Then considered action can systematically sort out the problem, at least as best as possible – you cannot wind the clock back. Finally, attention can turn not only to the lessons to be learnt (so as not to repeat similar disasters), but also to anything positive that might come from the whole incident.

Think positive. The Chinese ideogram for crisis consists of two characters: the first one means 'severe danger', the second means 'opportunity'. Enough said. Thereafter, you need to keep things in proportion. A crisis may impose stresses and strains, and surviving the occasional one is part of most jobs – though working so that they do not occur is perhaps even more important. As Anton Chekhov said, 'Any idiot can face a crisis – it's the day to day living that wears you out.'

If things are left late or ill-thought out (the two often go together), then time is used up in a hasty attempt to sort things out at short notice. This tends to make any task more difficult and is compounded by whatever day-to-day responsibilities are current at the time. If you can acquire the habit of thinking ahead – a system, as referred to above, will help you do this – then you are that much more likely to see when a start really needs to be made on something.

Some people find that to 'see' the pattern of future work and tasks in their mind's eye is difficult. One invaluable aid to this is the planning or wall chart. This enables you to create a picture of activities, and the time spans are very much clearer as you scan such a chart than when flicking through the pages of a diary. Charts come in all shapes and sizes: some are for the current year and are, effectively, large diaries; others are ruled for specific tasks, and others still are designed for you to create the detail. The large ones come with a variety of stickers to help highlight what is important; others are magnetic and can provide a permanently updatable guide to your schedule.

Whatever you do to document things, however, the key is to get into the habit of thinking ahead – at the same time and without disrupting the current day's workload. Anticipating problems and spotting opportunities can make a real difference to the way you work in the short term.

Spend time to save time

Whatever actions you might consider taking to keep yourself well organised – and there are many – they tend to fall into two categories: ones simple to implement, that only take a moment, and those that inherently take some time to set up, and perhaps some time thereafter to acquire as a retained working habit. If you limit yourself to the former, you will never maximise your time management effectiveness. So, returning to an earlier example, that of saying 'It's quicker to do it myself', in the short term the sentiment is often correct. It is quicker for you to do it, but this is only true at the moment something occurs.

Suffice it to say that this is an area that needs to become a sort of reflex. Every time you find yourself taking action based on this premise, stop and think for a moment whether you are doing the right thing. Is there a longer-term route that would be more useful? The more you do this, the more time you will save and the more you will be able to do it. There is a virtuous circle here. It stands some thought. Become determined not to be caught in the trap implicit here, and you are on a track that will save you a great deal of time in future. This more considered approach leads logically to the next topic.

Taking time to think

At the end of the training film *Time to Think*, the main character, a manager who has come to grips with managing his time better, is sitting in his office. A colleague comes into the outer office and begins to walk past the secretary to see him. The secretary stops him, says her manager is busy and suggests he makes an appointment to see him later. He looks past her at the manager sitting in his office (visible behind a glass partition) and says: 'But he's not doing anything...' Immediately the secretary replies that: 'He's thinking; now do you want to see him this afternoon or...' This incident makes a good point.

As a general rule it is true to say that the higher up the hierarchy of an organisation you go, you are expected to spend more time thinking, planning and decision making and less doing other things. It is also often true that the thinking, the planning and the idea generation that goes into a job are usually the most important things to be done in that job.

And what is the most difficult kind of time to keep clear and have sufficient of? Time to think will rank high. Make no mistake: many jobs demand a degree of creativity and this is something that is as important to a small change of approach or system as it is to some more radical development. My work in training seems to indicate that the pressurised workplace is one in which it is increasingly difficult to be creative. Giving yourself more time to think creatively, both alone and within a team, may be one of the most important things effective time management can do for you. Go back to your analysis of your time, or better

still your time log if you did one (if not you should) and see how
these activities show up. Are they getting the time they need and
deserve or are they squeezed out by other pressures and the
things that are more obviously urgent? I suggested earlier using
the breakdown of your time and tasks as a guide for a more ideal
breakdown. Make sure that you set your sights on creating
sufficient thinking time – perhaps above all – and that the action
you take to achieve this is not offset by unnecessary crises.
Without something approaching the ideal in this area, all your
objectives may be in jeopardy.

Be prepared to say 'no'

This is very much a first principle, and it needs some resolve to
carry it through, so it is as well to have it in mind throughout
your reading of the remainder of this book. Everyone has to
accept that they cannot do everything. This must be taken
literally because there may be an almost infinite amount to do in
any job that has some kind of inherent innovative or creative
nature to it. Many people could just go on listing more and more
things to do, not all equally important but deserving of a place on
their 'To do' list nevertheless. Even if your job is not like this, you
certainly have to accept that you are not going to do everything
when you want. Both in terms of quantity and priority you are
going to have to say 'no' to some things. It is worth considering
here not so much what you leave out but whom you say 'no' to.
For instance, you may have to turn down:

- **Colleagues. What is involved here can vary and if there
  is a network of favours, with everyone helping everyone
  else, you do not want to let it get out of hand either way.
  Turn down too much and you end up losing time
  because people are reluctant to help you. Do everything
  unquestioningly and you may be seen as a soft touch
  and will end up doing more than your share. So balance**

and timing are the keynotes here; you do not have to do everything that crops up in this way instantly.

- Subordinates. Here they cannot tell you to do things, and while they need support, this must not get out of hand.
- Your own boss. Working with a boss who does not have enough to do, or who expects everything to be done instantly just because he or she is the boss, can play havoc with the best intentions of time management. You may need to regard it as your mission to educate your boss and need to conduct a campaign of persuasion and negotiation to keep any unreasonable load down.

With all of these you need to resolve to think before you agree, and to turn down some potential involvements even though they might be attractive to you. But this is not all; the most difficult person to say 'no' to may well be yourself. There are always many reasons for saying 'yes' to things: you do not wish to offend others, you want to do whatever it is, you do not think about the way a new thing impinges on the current workload, etc. We all have our weak points in this regard and must beware of our own tendencies where they lead us away from priorities. Resolve to be firm with others. Saying 'no' is a fundamental time saver. It was well put by Charles Spurgeon: 'Learn to say no; it will be more use to you than to be able to read Latin.'

To be, or not to be (perfect)

Most people in a job they care about want to do things well (if you were not in that category you would probably not have picked up this book). But I digress – and am in danger of wasting your time! Some people take this further and are perfectionists. Now there is a place for this, and I would certainly not advocate that anyone adopts a shoddy approach to their work. There is, however, a dichotomy here, one well summed up in a quotation from Robert Heimleur, who said (perhaps despairingly): 'They didn't want it good, they wanted it on Wednesday.' The fact is it takes time to achieve perfection, and in any case, perfection may not always be strictly necessary. Things may need to be undertaken carefully, thoroughly, comprehensively, but we may not need to spend time getting every tiny detail perfect. This comes hard to those who are naturally perfectionists, and it is a trait that many have at least about some things, but it is necessary to strike a balance. The key balance to be struck is between quality – the standard to which things are done – and cost and time. It is one that needs to be consciously struck.

There is always a trade-off here, and it is not always the easiest thing to achieve. Often a real compromise has to be made. Cost is often key in this. It would be easy to achieve the quality of output you want in many things, but only if cost were no object. And in most jobs, budget considerations rank high. It is useful to get into the way of thinking about things in these terms, and doing so realistically so that you consider what is necessary as well as (or instead of?) what is simply desirable or ideal. In doing this there is one key factor that needs to be built in: a significant (and sometimes the largest) cost is your time.

For some, this is easy to cost. People like accountants or consultants will charge for their time by the day or hour and this makes them sensitive to just what costs are involved. In an organisation it is not just a question of dividing your salary to produce an hourly cost; you have to allow the many other costs of your being there. Factors will include everything from your office and office supplies to the cost of support – your secretary, for example, if you have one – and, of course, the cost of other benefits you receive in addition to salary.

It is worth your making this kind of calculation; the resultant figure may surprise you and it is a useful benchmark when considering many things in managing your time – whether you should make a journey, hold or attend a meeting and so on. Let me repeat, make sure by all means that what must be done to perfection is done in a way that achieves just that. Otherwise make sure you always keep in mind the balance to be struck between quality, cost and time. If you do not over-engineer quality seeking a standard that is not in some instances necessary or desirable, then you will surely save time.

Work smarter not longer

The answer to productivity in your job is not to work longer and longer hours. This may seem like a contradiction in terms. Surely if you put in more hours you will achieve more as a result? Yes, of course the direct answer to that is that you will. The point, however, is that there are limits. We all have the 24-hour day in common (unless there are creatures bending their tentacles to time management problems in Alpha Centauri). This is unchangeable and the amount of time we have to work with is finite.

It seems to be one of life's rules that jobs that are interesting do not allow a strictly nine-to-five attitude; in part, this is probably why they are interesting, so I am not advocating this. After all, you get out what you put in and working hard must make a difference. But it is here that another balance must be struck for most people: that between work and home and outside interests and commitments. If you overdo the work, the other things – and they are all important – suffer. What is more, damage, if damage is done, is insidious. You may not be aware of a difficulty until it is too late and begins to cause some real problems.

The answer is to seek to strike a balance; indeed, you may want to lay down some rules for yourself about this, specifying maximum hours to work, travel or spend on specific things. In addition, for those readers who are managers, remember that the work capacity of the team you control is very much greater than yours, so it always makes sense to take a team view of things rather than just opting to do more yourself. Finally, excessively long hours worked can be misunderstood and make it appear to others that you are inefficient, which is presumably the reverse of how you want to appear. Long hours will be necessary on some occasions, to complete a particular project, say, but in excess are likely to produce declining standards and run risks that make working smarter a much more attractive option. It is something to ponder (though not late into the night!) in order to make sure that you create a working pattern that is well balanced in this way.

Reward yourself

The final idea in this chapter can motivate you towards better time management and to ensure you continue to think about it as you work. It has already been said that time management is not easy, that it demands a concerted effort, so you need to motivate yourself and give yourself some real reasons to make it work. You need something more than just getting to the bottom of your in-tray. In any case, even the most effective person may never do this and, while what you achieve and how that is received is reward enough in some ways, what is wanted is something that is linked more specifically to your own success in managing your time.

It thus makes sense to set yourself specific time management goals and to link them to what that will do for you; to give yourself personal satisfaction so that you are very aware that succeeding in what you intend in time terms will make something else possible. Such rewards may be seemingly small and personal (they do not have to make much sense to anyone else), but nevertheless an example may make the point.

Take my work on this book. Having conceived and agreed the project, and this necessitates some time, the work falls into a number of stages: research and planning what the book will contain, structuring it (deciding the sections and sequence of points within each), actually writing it and final editing before the manuscript is sent to the publishers. Having discovered portable computers, I like to have some written work to do when I travel, and an overseas trip tends to contain quite a number of hours that can then be put to good use – on the flight and during otherwise wasted moments. Now the research and planning stage is difficult to do on the move as I need too many papers and too much space, so if I can complete that and have such a task at the writing stage as I start a trip then this gives me a manageable project to take with me. So, completing the initial work in time to fit in with a trip in this way becomes a private goal and the reward is that I have the right sort of task to accompany me on my travels. This may seem inconsequential but the point about it is that it is significant to me, and that is what matters.

If you can think in this kind of way and give yourself some sort of reward – better still a number of them – then your attention will remain focused on what time management can do for you. A major outcome of good time management is the ability to fit in projects that might otherwise be delayed, curtailed or omitted. Make such a pet project your reward, work out what is necessary in other areas to achieve it and you are just that much more likely to achieve what you want.

Everything reviewed so far will help you create a better basis for becoming more efficient at time management. In particular it will help you to adopt the right attitudes in terms of the overall approach to your work, and in terms of specific areas of activity. Like so much that we approach with good intentions, thinking that an attitude makes sense is still a little way from implementing the principles and techniques it dictates. In real life, good intentions have a habit of deserting you at particular moments in favour of expediency – or panic! It may be easier to adopt a trigger to memory rather than a more all-embracing intention. Saying that you will say 'no' to more requests may be difficult to apply consistently. However, some people find that resolving to count from 1 to 10 before accepting unwelcome and avoidable requests without due consideration does work. Rather than being rushed into a 'yes', they are able to give a considered response, perhaps one that has the intention of avoiding the involvement. Of course, nothing like this is infallible. However, if such a ploy reduces this kind of acceptance in any sort of worthwhile way, then it is useful, and other areas may be susceptible to similar thinking. All this will be made more effective if you and your work are essentially organised. In the next chapter we turn to the various ways of putting some order into the mess of reality.

3

Getting (and staying) organised

Despair is the price one pays for setting oneself
an impossible aim.

Graham Greene

Organisation and time management go together. Being well
organised creates the right time environment. Poor organisation
is insidious; everything takes just a little bit more time than it
should and this adds up day by day, inevitably reducing
effectiveness. This is true of even minor faults or omissions
which, duplicated across a number of activities, can together
have a significant effect and dilute efficiency. At worst, a lack of
organisation causes real, even debilitating, problems. The poorly
organised person:

- **cannot locate papers and information easily;**
- **allows muddle to enter their diary, sometimes to the
  point of double-booking;**
- **is inclined to 'task hop', moving between tasks in an
  attempt to meet many and conflicting deadlines,
  completing things erratically;**

- is late and ill-prepared for meetings;
- allows paperwork to proliferate;
- has no clear priorities;
- works in a mess;
- communicates poorly and keeps inadequate records.

As a result, they end up duplicating effort, wasting time, missing deadlines, and delivering inadequate or insufficient results, even after having apparently put in the time and effort required. Worse still in some ways, such poor performance is both visible to, and affects, others. Colleagues whose work overlaps with such a person are inconvenienced, the perpetrator collects a reputation for unreliability and not only is work affected but so are things such as personal promotion prospects.

Now all this is, I am sure, not painting a picture of you (the hopelessly disorganised will surely not pick up a book like this). But most of us will see a small part of ourselves in this kind of picture. You need little imagination to see how even some of the above can have the wrong kind of impact; and maybe, in some instances, memory confirms this view better than imagination!

It is all very well to stress the disadvantages of being disorganised, but how do you get, and stay, organised? The key, touched on in the last chapter, is having a plan. So we will return to that, looking not only at creating the plan but also at working the plan. Beyond this there are numerous different factors that contribute positively to a state of organisation: next we look at an unashamed mixture of them. Some are simple ideas, though they can have a significant influence nevertheless. Others are more fundamental. All perhaps need some thought to fit them to your existing methods of working, but many can also readily become habits so that you stop wasting time thinking about their implementation. First, back to planning.

Work the plan

There is more to this than just recording a list of 'Things to do'. Tasks must be noted in the right kind of way and the way you review the list can usefully follow a pattern. One such is the so-called LEAD system, with the letters of the word 'lead' standing for:

- **List the activities. This must be done comprehensively, though in note form as you do not want the list to become unmanageable.**
- **Estimate how long each item will take, as accurately as possible.**
- **Allow time for contingency as things always have a potential for taking longer than your best estimate; also allow time for regular tasks, the ongoing things that go on as a routine day by day.**
- **Decide priorities. This is a key, and one of the most important aspects of time management for anyone.**

Scan the plan, reviewing it overall probably once a day. (When I am in my office I like to do this at the end of each day, updating in the light of what has gone on during the day, followed by a quick review at the start of the next day when the mail arrives. But what matters is that what you find suits you.)

This process should become a routine. What other action may be necessary will depend on the pattern of your day and work. Something cropping up during the day may be either thought about and added to the list at the time or simply put on one side to be incorporated into the plan at the next review. I find the ubiquitous yellow sticky paper pads useful (like 3M's Post-it Notes) – whatever did we do before these existed? They can be used to make a brief note of something, appended to your planning sheet and then incorporated in permanent form later.

This review and recording cycle is the heartland of time management. Proprietary systems set it out in particular ways, sectioning things and arranging them under headings; and if this helps that is fine, but many find their own simpler system works perfectly well. A sheet ruled into a number of spaces or the use of a second colour, or both, can make what may well be a full list easier to follow. If items are reliably listed and the list conscientiously reviewed then you will keep on top of things and certainly nothing should be forgotten.

Batch your tasks

The trouble with so many jobs (most?) is that the list of things to do is itself apt to get unmanageable – unless the tasks are batched. An overriding principle of good time management is to batch your tasks. Here again the proprietary systems all have their own methodology, but what works best for you is the only measure. I am inclined to believe that what is more important than the precise configuration of the system here is the number of categories; three or four are ideal simply because that is manageable. It does not matter too much what you call them:

- **PRIORITY;**
- **IMPORTANT;**
- **ACTION NOW;**
- **OBTAIN MORE INFORMATION;**
- **READING.**

These are some of the options (and there are those who manage perfectly well with A, B and C). You will also need FILE and may consider other action categories such as TELEPHONE, WRITE, DISCUSS (perhaps divided into categories such as e-mails or reports), and similar ones that are particular to your business and your role in it, such as PROPOSALS, QUOTATIONS and the names of products, departments or systems. Some of the implementation of this necessarily comes under the section on paperwork. The important thing at this stage is to work out how many and what titles of batches suit you, and that this and the way you arrange your desk are not in conflict. A manageable number of batches of this sort can, if you wish, link physically to filing trays on your desk or some distinguishing mark on files themselves. (Incidentally, beware of colour-coding office-wide systems – a significant proportion of people are colour-blind.) One grouping, which can logically be commented on at this point, is events, most often appointments, which routine use of a diary can automatically batch together.

Use your diary effectively

A good clear diary system is a must. Many formal systems combine the conventional diary with their sophisticated version of the 'Things to do' list. One thing that certainly works well, and which a loose-leaf system allows, is to have at one opening of a binder a convenient complete picture of your day, showing both appointments and things to do.

Confusion is caused in many offices over what constitutes the master diary. A desk diary often lives on the secretary's desk, another in the executive's pocket and sometimes there is more duplication such as with a wall planner or computer system. This needs to be clear, and where appropriate, necessitates regular updates between the executive and the secretary, who must clearly both communicate and have an understanding about who does what. Small things have an effect on efficiency. The diary should:

- **Show full details, certainly full enough to be clear. An entry that reads 'R B Lunch' tells you little – where it is, at what time it is, can you be contacted while you are out, how long will it last, and, not least, are you even going to remember in three weeks' time to whom R B refers? Worse, I know of a case where all it said in someone's diary was 'Oxford', across two days. He was** away, presumably staying at a hotel, and had only told his family to contact him via his office. When one of his children was involved in a car accident, it took two days before the message reached him. His diary was a copybook example of clarity thereafter.

- Show how long is set aside for things (this will help decide what else can be fitted in).
- Be completed in pencil so that alterations can be made without creating an illegible mess.

A planner element within a diary is very useful. Certainly I could not operate without one, and anyone who operates in a way that necessitates taking an overview of a period and seeing how things relate one to another is likely to find it invaluable. Perhaps the most important and useful difference between just an appointments diary and a time management system is if it is used to schedule all (or most) of the working time rather than just appointments. The two additions are: tasks, actually setting aside time to work on a specific project, and thinking time, so that planning and creative work is not carried out, as so often happens, only in gaps that are left between appointments and meetings. If this is done – leaving some space for the unexpected and any reactive part of the work, and linked to the concept of the rolling plan, you will stay much more organised and better able to judge how things are progressing, whether deadlines will be met and tasks completed.

Two final points. The diary is a vital tool, to be guarded and treated with respect. It is also, therefore, a good place to keep other key information, telephone numbers and other data you need at your fingertips, provided you do not overburden it so that it becomes too thick and unmanageable.

The computer, and a variety of electronic personal organisers, are taking over some of these activities. Often this works well. Being able to set a meeting with six colleagues, some in different cities, at the touch of a button on a networked system may well save time. But for many people a personal diary or planner, usable anywhere there is a pencil, will always be a part of what helps them work effectively. Certainly, the thinking that needs to be applied to diary organisation is the same however the information involved may be recorded.

Schedule appointments with care

Appointments, transactions with other people, take up a major amount of many executives' time. Exactly when you programme them makes a real difference to your productivity. Allow sufficient time; one appointment running into another always causes problems. And always schedule a period of time, in other words, a finishing time as well as a start time. It is impossible to do this with 100 per cent accuracy, but it helps. Think about:

- **The potential for interruptions (an early meeting, before the office switchboard opens, may take less time because there are fewer interruptions).**
- **The location (where it is geographically makes a difference). A meeting room may be better than your office, especially if you need to move what you are working on just before it starts.**
- **Timing that makes it inevitable that it continues into lunch or a drink at the end of the day.**
- **Timing that restricts your ability to schedule other appointments, in the way that something mid-morning could mean there is not sufficient time to fit in another meeting before it, or after it and before lunch.**

And take especial care with gatherings that involve more than one person. You have to be accommodating here, but do not always consider others' convenience before your own – it is you who will suffer. Always record appointments clearly in the diary.

While considering when to schedule appointments, it may be worth a slight digression to make a point about the most fundamental level of scheduling: that affected by your personal time clock. There is a serious, and useful, point to be made here. I am a morning person and try to allow for this in how I operate. Accommodating your nature in this respect is one of many areas where you will never achieve perfection, but that is no reason to ignore it; get things mostly right and you will be more productive and waste less time.

Clear your desk

There are those who are in no danger of boosting the sales of furniture polish; their desks are totally covered with piles of paper and the wooden surfaces never see the light of day. These are the same people who if asked about it, always reply, 'But I know where everything is.' They mean it too and some of them are right. But, and it is a big but, this kind of disorder rarely goes with good time management. It pays to be neat. It pays you and it may also pay the organisation for which you work. This is worth another slight digression. If you are employed by a large organisation, you are not indispensable. Sorry, but it is true. What is more, it is incumbent in your responsibilities that you protect the continuity of operations and this includes thinking about what happens if you are, for any reason, not there. Even a short absence by someone on sick leave, say, can cause havoc. It takes others a while to locate things you were working on and, because of the difficulty, matters can be disrupted or delayed. Worse perhaps from your point of view, when you return and other people have been rifling through your system, you are not going to be able to find anything.

So resolve to keep your desk tidy. This means having a clear, and clearly labelled, system, one that is likely to be more specific than an 'In' and 'Out' tray and is reasonably intelligible to others. Having said all that, I recognise that there is a need in many people to have things visible, a belief that out of sight is out of mind and that this may lead to things being forgotten. This can be accommodated in part by your diary and planning system, which can link to and identify where things are – in files or whatever – but still the need is there. Frankly, I share it; there are certain kinds of thing I want visibly to hand and I am not as confident of having my fingers on everything unless that is so. One solution to this is to have a tray (or something bigger if necessary) that contains current project files. I have this to one side of my desk, and the top item in it is a list of those files that are there – because it is a changing population – which helps me check quickly if I am up to date with things. The list, which is in a transparent plastic folder, also records the status of projects and I find this very useful. Thus I believe it is possible to accommodate both views realistically; having key things to hand but keeping your desk clear. For most ordinary mortals it is a constant battle to keep things tidy, a battle that ebbs and flows, but one worth keeping a continuous eye on.

Avoid 'cherry picking'

Your approach to time management needs to be systematic. Some of the techniques that have been discussed here demand habit and a consistent approach. Some people are good at this, they make the plan, they list the priorities, they have a good diary and time system and are careful about their decisions and work practice in terms of how they affect the way they use time. But they then make one significant mistake that negates all this effort: they cherry pick. That is, they keep picking out jobs, possibly for one of the reasons that was reviewed earlier, such as because they like them. Whatever the reason, they keep rethinking their priorities and deciding that something else must be done first. They can spend so much time doing this that the plan never settles and time is not spent primarily actioning it. Of course, a time plan is not static. It does need regular fine-tuning, but this must not become an excuse for not sticking to it. If your plan is reviewed regularly, and if the decisions made about it are good ones, then you can stick to it and will make more progress through the work list by doing so. Have confidence in your plan and resist being sidetracked by anything and it will work better for you.

Use abstracts

No one needs reminding of the amount of reading there is to do in most jobs. For some it is very important to keep up to date with the technical area their job involves, for others management processes themselves are worth regular study. In both cases, the first task is to decide which, from the very many references published, should command your attention. This first selection exercise can be time-consuming in itself before you actually study anything individually.

But here help is at hand. In most fields it is possible to subscribe to what are called abstract services. These are not expensive and from them you receive a regular list of what has been published on a given subject. Such a list does not just list the title of articles or papers (and books), but who wrote them, sometimes details of the author and, most important, a synopsis of the content. It is this latter point that lets you select with reasonable accuracy those items you judge you want to look at in more detail. You can then either turn up the source and read the item in full (scanning it first, no doubt) or, in some cases, the service will provide – for a small fee – a copy of a particular article without your having to purchase the full magazine or journal in which it appears.

If the thought of this facility appeals to you then you may want to check locally what services are available. Typically, they will come from libraries, colleges, trade associations and professional bodies (management institutes may be able to help you), business schools and the like. Many can now be delivered by e-mail. If you find something that offers a service that appears to suit you then it is perhaps worth taking out a subscription for a short period and see whether it does save you time. If it does, and if it also helps you find information you might otherwise miss, it can then be economic to continue, in which case you have another continuing time saver on your side.

The internet

The internet provides a source of almost infinite information, one that can be accessed quickly and, once mastered, easily. To take a very simple example, where once you might have obtained background information about a company by sending off for its annual report, now you can view its website, see the report verbatim and dig deeper for more specific or updated information. And this can be done at minimal cost without leaving your workstation.

Beware, however, surfing the internet is a major source of distraction. One thing leads all too easily to another and it can be tempting to spend a minute or two more 'just in case you can access something better or more specific', and then a minute or two more again. Be warned, some real discipline may be necessary here – for yourself and perhaps on behalf of others whom you manage. *Note:* another new word has entered the language: cyberloafing. Not only is a vast amount of time wasted by people surfing the internet in ways that have nothing to do with work, some of it is so inappropriate that it has become grounds for dismissal. Avoid it; and resist too the social pressure involved in circulating jokes and other material by e-mail.

Highlight key facts

Amongst the mass of paperwork you have to read, file, keep or pass on, there are some things contained in it that stand out. When you go back to a specific document you will likely have a keyword, heading or section in mind and finding this can lead you straight to the key facts without combing through all the detail. But you need to be able to find the prompt element fast.

Highlighting things on paper is easy with a fluorescent highlighting pen. It is a small point perhaps, but one or more of these in your desk drawer is a great little time saver. They work well and any section, heading or word in a document marked with one really stands out; you cannot flick through a stack of papers and miss a page with a mark. They lead you to essentials, and I for one would not be without them. Like the yellow sticky sheets popularised by 3M, they are now a part of office life we cannot imagine not being there. If for some reason these are not in your desk drawer, get some soon and give them a try. I predict you will quickly be hooked and become a regular user – they are not expensive and they may save a few moments every day.

Insist on quality

Quality has always mattered, and always will, but is currently enjoying something of a special emphasis with Quality Management having been elevated into a major issue, often under the name Total Quality Management. This is no bad thing as anything that emphasises so important an aspect of corporate performance is all to the good.

Look at this for a moment on a more local scale. Consider your office, your department. Does it do a good job? Now you may well answer, 'Of course', but how do you really know? Ask: Are there sufficient performance standards? Are you aiming specifically at achieving particular levels in all activities? And so on.

For example, in the area of customer service, a bank may specify that no more than three customers should be in a single queue, that each should receive a greeting as they are attended to and that the customer's name should be used at the end of the transaction as they depart. Small points perhaps, but it is the summation of such points that add up to the standard of customer service that they intend to provide. Such standards are designed not simply to specify what should happen, but to make it more certain that the standards are achieved in practice. If you think banks are a poor example, I agree!

You may have noticed (from your own time log?) how much time is sometimes spent sorting out things that have gone wrong. And this need not mean very wrong, but just falling short of the ideal by a small margin. Consider the bank example again. If customers are kept waiting just a little too long some of them will comment on the fact, the cashier will apologise and perhaps explain, and the transaction will then proceed, usually without further problem. But it will take a little longer than it would otherwise, and with many hundreds of people seen each day at the counter this matters, not least to other customers whose wait is increased.

This is a simple example, but similar things will apply in your office. If you and your team get things right, and know what is necessary to get it right, then things will take less time, first because tasks will be performed efficiently, second because there will be less time wasted in any disruption caused by performance to a lesser standard.

Quality is a great friend of good time management. You should think about the standards of work with which you are involved, and clarify this area if necessary. Further, if there are moves within your organisation to embrace the likes of Total Quality Management, this will be worth supporting. There are set-up costs and time needs to be invested also, but the equation is likely to work. Such initiatives will save time. 'Do it right and the time it takes will be less' is a good general principle and can be applied to many areas of work. Quality saves time.

Action or investment

Few people are bad time managers because they are idle. Certainly most of those with an interest in time management are busy people, but they are not getting everything done, or everything done thoroughly and on time. And the thing that gets neglected most is investment time; this is time taken now to ensure improvements or results in future – the planning and analysis and other such activities necessary to make progress in any area.

Categorising on your plan which category of time you are scheduling will help create a balance (it has already been mentioned that diary and 'To do' lists should schedule tasks – some evolve a code to differentiate between different sorts of task in this way). Thus the plan will show whether time is to be taken up with people (appointments, meetings, etc) or tasks (and whether they are action or investment-orientated). It will also allow for the unexpected. And this will be seen at a glance, maybe in the double opening of a loose-leaf book, so that fine-tuning can take place if necessary. After all, time planning should be a guide and assist the way you work, not a straitjacket that restricts you.

If you have a good feel for how much of your job should be spent in action time and how much in investment time, then you will be better able to maintain the balance you need, using the techniques of time management to create the working pattern you want. Time management is, and should be regarded as, a personal tool, something that you use to help you and not a standard approach that you must adopt in order to be efficient.

A good personal assistant (or secretary)

There is an old story told about a secretary to a much-travelling and very senior executive. Asked by someone one day if he could see him, she replied that she was sorry but he was in Singapore. 'Abroad again', he replied, 'He's always overseas. Tell me, who does all his work while he's away?' She looked him straight in the eye and answered without hesitation: 'The same person who does it when he's here.' Some personal assistants or secretaries perhaps have such authority, but while they are a panacea no more than the time management system sold on the basis that it will reorganise your life effortlessly is, he or she can help. For those who have one, a good PA can be not only the recipient of some of your delegation, he or she can also act as a regular prompt to good time management and take a genuinely active role in organising you, or your whole department. The emphasis here is on 'good', so the first job is to find the right one for you; and then, as we will see, work with him or her to create the end result you want.

The characteristics of the ideal PA are many and varied. As well as typing, and sometimes shorthand, skills, he or she must be familiar with an increasing array of office technology. But what of time management? Whether a person has a natural or acquired organisational ability is difficult to assess at an interview, as is whether he or she really cares about such things. If you can do so, however, and only appoint a candidate who has characteristics of this sort, then you will have a real asset on board in your battle to win the time war. Ask any questions you can think of that will give you information in this area, particularly about past experience in managing the diary and appointments of previous employers. This is also something to check when taking up references; it is always worth doing in almost any recruitment situation. At this level, a phone call – with the permission of the candidate – to a last employer is probably the quickest check. It will be likely to give the best information anyway as people are reluctant to take the time or make the commitment to put references in writing.

There are two other important characteristics in a PA that you should seek. First, the ability to work your way. This is important as there may be existing procedures and systems, as well as management style, that you need your PA to fit in with; on the other hand, always be ready to learn from him or her. There is no monopoly on good ideas, and in this area you should be on the look out for ideas from any source, the only criterion being that the ideas are useful. A good PA will also have sufficient 'weight' or clout, that is, he or she must be able to stand up for you with colleagues and others, to say 'no' on your behalf and to make requests on your behalf – and make it stick. Achieve this and your attempts to control your time will have a permanent ally, one who will work with you to achieve what you want and who will, at best and with experience, take an active role in the process.

Commonly today, PAs must be shared. This need not negate anything said here, though it might make being the senior partner a valuable position, one that allows you to influence the way things work. It will also compound the need for care in communication with a PA, to which we turn next.

Communicate with your personal assistant (or secretary)

It is no use having a good PA, one who is sympathetic to time management, and then not communicating with him or her. This is a classic example of something for which there is 'never time' but which, if you do find the time for it, will help you save much more time than this communication takes. Many executives start the day with a meeting with their PA, perhaps when the mail arrives in the morning. You must decide what suits you best and also work out a way of keeping in touch and up to date with your PA if you spend much time out of the office, though modern communications make this easier than once was the case.

Your PA must know how you work and what you have on the go at any particular time. And he or she should, if possible, share your view of priorities, knowing what you are prepared to be interrupted for, which things and people rate most time and attention, and what must be actioned first. You need to review and organise the diary together, and over time it helps if you explain what you are doing and why in order to pass on some of the detail beyond the letters and reports. Once a PA has some experience, more may well be possible. He or she can take the initiative on things, accompany you to certain meetings and ultimately run whole areas of your office life in a way that improves your utilisation of time dramatically. Find areas of real responsibility, let him or her look after them and make the decisions affecting them and it can pay dividends.

You must make it work. It is no good coming back to the office after a trip and complaining that things have not been completed or that you now have a string of time-wasting meetings in your diary, if your lack of communication has caused this situation. So, communicate clearly and regularly, and remember that this includes listening.

As a footnote to this point it should perhaps be mentioned that working with a PA necessitates that all the managerial techniques are brought to bear appropriately. This will include development, motivation and many more. A good relationship does not just happen, it demands some time up front – but the results can be very worthwhile.

Use a 'document parking' system

This point might equally have been listed under paperwork, but it is so useful a device that it deserves to come in here. Perhaps the best explanation begins with the problem it solves. You may have many things on the go at any one time, and in physical terms, they may consist of a single sheet of paper or a batch of correspondence. Many of them do not need action, or cannot be actioned immediately. This is what so often constitutes the ever-present overloaded Pending Tray. The net result is that you spend a great deal of time either shuffling through the heap to locate things, or checking things in there to see what you might, in time, do about them. The nature of some of the material makes the problem worse. Say one item can only be actioned when certain monthly performance figures are published at the end of the month, then to keep checking it may well be both time-consuming and useless as no action can be taken anyway.

Further, constant reviewing can achieve little in advance of knowledge of the figures.

If you suffer this sort of situation you need a parking place for such things, somewhere safe yet guaranteed to trigger prompt action at the appropriate moment. You need what is called a Prompt File (sometimes also called a Bring-Forward or, less elegantly, a Bring-Up File). This means you take an item and decide when you will be able to progress it. This may be at a specific time (when the monthly figures arrive) or it may not (just six weeks on, or longer, at the start of the next financial year). Then you simply mark it with the date on which you next want to see it and file it, with other similar items, in date order. Then forget it. Waste no more time even thinking about it. You do not have to, because every day your PA will check the file and bring anything marked with that day's date in to you with the morning mail. At which point you can either act or, occasionally, give it another date and move it forward.

A couple of provisos: first, you may want to limit the total quantity of items (or list them alphabetically) as something will happen occasionally that means you need to take action earlier than you thought, and you will need to retrieve an item from the file and action it ahead of the date you originally set. Second, you may want to link it to a diary note, especially if you have no PA. This is such a simple common-sense idea and everyone I know who runs one swears by it. If you do not already use this system, it takes very little time to set up. Why not give it a try?

Make use of checklists

How many times a week do you have to pause and think about how exactly to complete some routine task? Or you do it wrong or incompletely in respect of some detail? Even if you only have a few tasks to complete, checklists will save time, and save it both by preventing those pauses for thought and, more importantly, removing the necessity to do something again. Consider an example. Many companies have a form that is completed when a sales enquiry is received. Completing such a form does not only create a record and act as a prompt to further action, it can also act as a checklist, for instance reminding you to:

- **check the enquirer's job title as well as name;**
- **ask how they heard of the company or product;**
- **refer to an account number;**
- **check that you obtain any additional information such as credit details and as many more items as circumstances demand.**

Many such routine tasks are not always predictable; conversation with the customer may take all sorts of routes and it is easy to forget those questions that might be considered optional, or at least of lesser importance. So a checklist helps. This can be either a form (like a customer enquiry form) designed to act as a checklist as its completion proceeds, or a point of reference, literally just a note of what should be done. Some of these you may want to create for yourself and your department, others take the form of company 'standing instructions' and, despite often being categorised as 'yet another memo', may be well worth keeping. Many exist only on computer screens.

You may like to make a mental note to look in particular at things that provide assistance outside your own area of expertise. For instance, if you are a dunce with figures, do not throw out that checklist concerning the procedure to reclaim expenses. It might just help you keep track of how much money you've spent so that you can reclaim it, or at least avoid the wrath of an accountant whose system is being ignored – and save you some time.

Remember: this kind of documentation is clearly not only useful to record information, but the items listed also act as a prompt to remind you of necessary action. A plethora of such forms can be purchased as standard items or designed internally to do just what you want.

Directing the techniques at particular result areas

All the techniques mentioned in this chapter, and more no doubt, can help you become generally more time-efficient; effects can be targeted also. Everything you do in time management terms is designed to affect efficiency, effectiveness and productivity; to enable you to do more and to do everything better than would otherwise be the case, so as to achieve the results your job demands. But there are advantages to be gained en route to these ends, and these are useful in their own right. Bearing them in mind can help you adopt some of the methodology necessary to an organised way of working and make the whole process easier. Such advantages include:

- **Having a clear plan, knowing and having an overview of what must be done – the first step to successfully completing the tasks on your list. Such clarity will make adequate preparation more likely and this can reflect directly on achievement.**
- **Having a clear link between things to do and overall objectives is a sound recipe to keeping on track.**
- **Being better organised (eg, not wasting time looking for things).**
- **Your memory coping better with what you actually need to remember (the systems take care of some of this for you, and it is not necessary to keep everything in your head).**
- **Being better able to identify and concentrate on the essentials.**
- **Wasting less energy on irrelevancies.**
- **Making better decisions about how things should be done (and better business decisions generally).**
- **Better coordination of tasks (progressing certain things in parallel saves time).**

- Having a greater ability to cope with or remove distractions and interruptions.
- Cultivating the habit of greater self-discipline about time matters, which makes consistency of action progressively easier.
- A greater ability to cope with the unexpected and emergency elements of any job.

Any of these are useful, but some may be more useful to you than others, at least at a particular moment or stage. It may be useful to look for the particular advantage you want, wasting less energy on irrelevancies or, more specifically, attending fewer meetings, for example. Or you may wish to adopt methods that will have precisely the impact you want. This is not to say that all those listed above do not have a good general effect on productivity. They do. But they produce additional, and more personal advantage also. You will achieve more and get greater satisfaction from the results you achieve. In addition, you may have more time to develop what you do and how you do it, and motivate yourself and any staff you may have, all of which can potentially improve things still further. And it may remove some of the things that create the feeling that a job is 'hard work' (different from 'working hard'). In my experience, the latter is nearly always a prerequisite of success. You do not want tasks to constantly put you in mind of trying to nail jam to the wall when a little organisation will ensure they go smoothly.

This list of advantages makes both a suitable summary to this section and preliminary to all that follows. If you bear these and other advantages in mind they can help you implement specific changes with clear ends in mind.

Intermission... take a break

Another thing: time management is about... er, productivity... and er... effectiveness. So... it... that is...

Sorry, I had to take a break for a moment there. I went to get a cup of tea (another cup of tea, if I am honest; very nice too). This took maybe three or four minutes and I do not believe it extended the time taken to put the comments on this topic together. Indeed, the way they are presented was largely decided in some of that three or four minutes. After working on any intensive task for a while most people find their concentration flags; certainly mine does in writing. An occasional break is not a contradiction of the productivity you seek, it actually helps it. You return to your desk and your head is clearer; you feel refreshed and revived by stretching your limbs and can get back to the task in hand with renewed fervour.

This is particularly true of seemingly intractable tasks. Sometimes you can sit and puzzle about things for a long time and seem to get nowhere. After a break, as you start again, it suddenly seems clear – or at least clearer – and again time is saved as a result. Sometimes a break may be as simple as standing up and stretching, or making a cup of tea (for me no job goes well without a regular supply of tea). Or it may be that you can benefit from something that takes a bit longer – you go to lunch even though you originally planned to do that an hour later, or you go for a walk. At one time I shared an office with someone who did this – the office was opposite a park and he had a particular circuit that took about 10 minutes and was useful thinking time, perhaps being applied to something else apart from the job in hand. This made a break, yet was still productive. Alternatively, all you may need is simply to switch tasks for a moment, rather than stop work, in order to ring the changes.

In any event, a break is often much more productive than struggling on with a job when concentration is not adequate. Again, it is something to utilise consciously and a pattern of such activity can become a useful habit if not taken to extremes.

Something to think about perhaps. Remember Doug Kling's saying: 'Learn to pause... or nothing worthwhile will catch up with you.' Take a few minutes. It will test the idea. Me? I am going to have a bite of lunch before I even think about writing more; it will be more productive in the long run.

4

Combating the time wasters

The art of being wise is the art of knowing what
to overlook.

William James

Nothing is more annoying than... There is not anything half as
distracting...

Nothing is more annoying than being interrupted except
being interrupted unnecessarily – more than once. And, as you
may have noticed, it just happened to me – twice. Interruptions
can take many forms. People are behind many of them, in person
at your elbow, on the telephone or shouting from afar. Also
involved are emergencies, fire drills, computer malfunctions,
visits to the stationery cupboard, accepting deliveries, lunch,
coffee and what might be delicately called comfort breaks; all
take up time, usually more than they reasonably should.

In the previous chapter, clear and positive planning was
advocated and yet (this was touched on) however sensible that
sounds, however much you want to set a plan and follow it,
things seem to conspire to make it impossible. I recall reading a
survey somewhere that said that the average time a manager

spends working uninterrupted is less than 15 minutes. Many will endorse that all too easily. Interruptions and other time-wasting intrusions are endemic. You either collapse under the weight of them, becoming fatalistic and believing that they are inevitable and there is nothing that can be done to reduce them, or you go on the offensive. This may well be the most obvious example of the need not to let perfection be the enemy of the good, because you will always get some interruptions. But you can reduce their number; and, if you want to be effective at time management and reap the rewards, you must do so.

If you worked in a hermetically sealed room, safe and protected from the outside world, if you had no interactions with people and the telephone never rang, you would no doubt get a great deal more work done. But it would be a sterile environment and you would in many ways be less creative and less effective, because what you do in business draws strength from the various interactions and stimuli around you. And in any case, a sterile environment is simply not one of the options. So, the intention here is not to cut yourself off from the outside world completely or avoid legitimate interruptions, some of which can be positive. It is to minimise the real time wasters and replace some of them with more time-effective ways of achieving what we want.

The greatest time waster?

So, we start by looking at three important aspects of one of the greatest time wasters, certainly the greatest procrastinator: you. This is an area of habit and of human nature that needs fighting (the right word, I think) for there are things here that we tend to return to again and again, with time being frittered away on every occasion:

1.   **Do not put off the things you find difficult.** The time wasted here can occur in two ways. First, decision making is delayed, then implementation is delayed and

both let time leak away. Let us take a dramatic example. Imagine you manage a group of people, one of whom is performing badly. Action must be taken, and there are only ever three options here:

- put up with it (which is not to be recommended);
- develop or persuade the person to perform more effectively;
- dismiss the poor performer (or otherwise move them out).

The reasons for the poor performance may need checking, which can be difficult, so the temptation is to put it off – and time goes by. Or you decide that development of some sort is necessary and, if it is something you have to do, this is delayed – and time goes by. Or perhaps you decide it is a hopeless case and dismissal is the only solution. But no one really enjoys firing someone. It is difficult so you put it off, perhaps to try to think of the best way of doing it (there is no painless way). And throughout the entire process, the thought keeps coming to mind that 'maybe it will get better'. This kind of thinking can be all too common and you can probably equate it with many difficult tasks you have had to tackle.

Now it seems to be a sad fact that difficult things do not get easier if they are left for a while. Worse, in many cases, what starts out as a bit difficult rapidly becomes very difficult if left and often breeds additional problems along the way. Think again of the aforementioned scenario. What are the costs of continuing poor performance if things are allowed to run? And what is the nature of them? In other words, how else will things become affected? For example, if the poor performer is a salesperson the cost can be measured in the revenue of lost sales but, depending on the nature of the poor performance, may also be counted in terms of lost customer goodwill, which might be even more costly in the long term.

So, do not put off the things, whatever they may be,

large or small, that you find difficult. Of course, the thought, consideration, checking, or whatever needs to be done, must be done and in many contexts should not be skimped, but once you are able to make the decision or take the action, or both, then there is merit in doing so. Watch out for any tendency you have in this respect; controlling it can save considerable time and aggravation.

2. **Do not put off the things you do not like.** There is a difference between what you find difficult and what you simply do not like. The likely effect of delay and avoidance of tasks is very similar to that referred to above, and I will not give a similar example here, but the motivation is different, though not less powerful. There may be numerous reasons for disliking doing some thing: it involves something else you do not like (perhaps something that necessitates a visit to a regional office, something that will take up a whole day and involves an awkward journey) or, more often, the dislike is minor – it is just a chore. This is perhaps the chief reason why administration is so often in arrears. It is boring and there are other things to do and... you know the feeling.

   The only real help here is self-discipline and a conscious effort in planning what you do to make sure that such things do not get left out and that this, in turn, does not lead to worse problems. Some flagging system to highlight things on your list may act as a psychological prompt. Experiment here to see if it makes a difference.

   If all this seems minor and you disbelieve the impact of this area, it is likely that any time log exercise you undertake will confirm the danger. Again, it seems simple, but the correct approach can save a worthwhile amount of time.

3. **Beware of your favourite tasks.** This is potentially even more time wasting than putting off things that you do not like or find difficult, and often the most difficult to accept. But many people spend a disproportionate amount of time on the things they like doing best – and perhaps also do

best. This is perfectly natural and there are various reasons for it. An important one is that any concentration on what you like is what seems to produce the most job satisfaction. This is fine if that satisfaction comes simply from doing whatever it is and the thing itself is necessary, but the danger is that you may be prone to over-engineering, doing more than is necessary, putting in more time and sometimes producing a standard of quality or excellence that is just not necessary.

But there can be more sinister reasons for this practice. For example, it may be because you:

– are using one task to provide an excuse to delay or avoid others (the difficult things, perhaps), telling yourself, with seeming reason, that you are too busy to get to them;
– are concerned about delegating (a subject to which we return) and worry that a task is not a candidate for this, so you go on doing it yourself and go on over-engineering;
– find the work conditions of one thing too tempting, such as a low-priority job that involves visiting an attractive city new to you – something that is compounded by the opposite being true of the priority task;
– find some aspect of possible over-engineering fun, such as spending hours devising a graphic representation of some figures when something simpler would meet the case just as well;
– do not know how to go about something else and use the familiar as an excuse for delay or inappropriate delegation.

All these and more can cause problems in this way. It is frankly all too easy to do, we are all prone to it, probably all do it to some extent and thus all have to be constantly on our guard against it. Usually it continues because it is easy not to be consciously aware that it is happening. The answer is to really look, and look honestly, as you review your tasks and your regular work plan for examples of this happening. Better still, look for examples of where it might happen and make sure that it does not. Of all the points in this book, I would rate this as in the top few best potential time savers for most people. Do not be blind to it – it is so easy to say, 'But I don't do that.' Check it out and see how much time you save. And, who knows, maybe some of the extra things you can then fit in will become tomorrow's favourite tasks.

Self-generated interruptions can be surprisingly time-consuming and are one of the surprises that often emerge from a personal time log. It is easy to be blind to them and, at the risk of being repetitive, it is logical to watch for these before the ones involving other people. Not that those are insignificant; read on.

Why uncomfortable is good

Everyone has some difficult things to do, and this was referred to in point 1) in the previous section; indeed they can link to things you don't like in point 2). There is another category, one that in a sense combines the two factors here and is worth a moment before we move on. Such may even highlight a simple way of improving performance and results from what might be called the 'discomfort zone'.

In the modern workplace being hard pressed is the norm. Corporate culture, finance, staffing, customer and market demands, competitive pressure and the administrative burden that underpins it all – all this and more contribute. There is an irresistible temptation to search for panaceas, one straightforward approach that will improve or guarantee business results, when realistically any such magic formulae are often well disguised – as hard work. That said, there may be one approach to how you work where attention to it, and resolve about it, can positively affect many key activities.

To exploit this you first need to be honest about yourself.

Take me: despite being, I like to think, knowledgeable about, and practiced in, various areas of management and business practice, there are, I admit, some tasks where my approach falters. It is difficult to admit this – damn it, I have written a book about time management! – but I have been known to procrastinate. Where does this happen most often? On examination that is easy to say: it is when something is not just difficult (I enjoy a challenge!), but when it is a particular kind of difficult – when it is actually uncomfortable. This may be conscious: for example, there are things about my computer skills that need attention – I know that my skills have gaps and am conscious that it is easy to get into deep trouble, yet I put off taking action because it is kind of awkward. Everyone probably has things that prompt such thoughts, and then make delaying action more likely.

Alternatively, there are things where avoidance is a more subtle process, where we try to rationalise and do not actually accept that our procrastination is significant, sometimes refusing to see the reality at all. As a result certain things are left unaddressed and performance can deteriorate directly as a result. And all because of some woolly, half-buried and perhaps repressed feeling that taking action will be an uncomfortable or embarrassing experience. Let's return to an example from a page or two back that affects many people who manage others.

When performance is inadequate

Imagine: one of your staff is performing under par. This might be anything from not hitting sales targets to more minor matters; the details are unimportant. One thing is clear – it demands action. The rewards are considerable, let us say, and further are easily recognised. Dealing with it will produce more sales, higher productivity – and more, depending on the precise details. Yet... with such things there can seem to be many reasons for delay. We think (or rather hope) that matters will get better. We wait for other things: the end of the month (bringing further figures or evidence) or a forthcoming appraisal (which we know means we cannot put it off later than that). More than anything we blame other things. We are busy, we have greater priorities (really?), or, even less convincingly, we are sorting out other problems – fire fighting.

It may be an uncomfortable truth, but the truth is we do not want to deal with it. We may be unsure how to do so, and that can be awkward. More likely we do know what to do, but know it will be awkward or embarrassing to do so; this is especially the case in some circumstances, for example where people managed may be senior or experienced. Addressing it will take us into the discomfort zone, and we would rather distance ourselves, busying ourselves elsewhere (with something we tell ourselves is more important!) and remaining safely outside this zone of personal difficulty.

The facts of the matter are usually clear, and can usually be dealt with if things are addressed directly. Poor performance is a good example. It is important, yet it is not complicated. Consider: essentially only three options are possible, you can:

1. Put up with the poor performance, and allow it to continue (which is surely something no one would defend or recommend).
2. You can address the problem determined to cure it, persuading or motivating someone to perform better; or training or developing him or her to do whatever it is better if poor performance is due to a shortfall in or lack of some skill or competence.
3. You can conclude, perhaps after option two has failed, that they will never get better and fire them (or otherwise move them to other areas of responsibility).

Both options two and three may be awkward. It is embarrassing to tell someone their performance is unacceptable, and most people would find firing someone worse. So, action is delayed.

Recognising reality

The situation here needs to be addressed head on. Such a situation is not a failing of logic, not a deficit of information or understanding, or anything else that mistakenly leads us away from the sensible and necessary course – it is a personal decision: we put avoiding personal discomfort above sorting out the problem and, very likely, delay makes the problem worse.

Before you say, 'But I never make that kind of decision', consider further. If this thinking is partly subconscious, then that is likely so because we push it into the back of our mind, refusing to really analyse what is occurring, or simply allowing other activity to create a blinding smokescreen. Now, thinking more constructively, which elements of your work are likely to run foul of this kind of avoidance technique? Other examples include:

- raising a difficult issue at a meeting (it gets put off rather than risking controversy or argument);
- cold calling in selling (many of us should do more, but it is not our favourite thing);
- networking (sounds good: we all hope to meet people at that conference we attend, then come out with one business card because we are not quite sure how to approach people. Worse the card is from whoever sat next to us, rather than for someone selected for a good reason);
- chasing debtors (we hate it, avoid it or do it half-heartedly and so cash flow suffers; yet we should all recognise that an order is not an order until the money is in the bank);
- follow-up (when someone, a customer or colleague, has said 'I'll think about it' how many times do we make one perfunctory phone call to be told they are in a meeting, then leave it so long that the moment passes because we are not quite sure what to say next time).

Such things are, to an extent, routine. Others may be more personal, linking to a particular skill or activity. For instance, avoiding presentations – even when they offer promotional opportunity, because you feel 'It's not really my thing'. Ditto other things, perhaps writing reports. Also avoiding sitting on a committee where you might make valuable contacts because meetings are in the evening and 'It's not fair on the family'.

You may well be able to extend the list in both categories (be honest, as I said at the beginning of this section).

Identifying opportunities

So, what do we conclude from this? There is a significant opportunity here.

You need to resolve to actively seek out uncomfortable situations. You need to see the discomfort zone as an attractive place to go. It is somewhere where you can achieve action and influence results, and often do so quickly and easily adding to the effectiveness of your time management. Additionally difficult situations may demand a creative solution and need constructive thought before action is taken. Indeed you need to go on seeking solutions.

After all, probably most people can identify with this feeling: you take some long overdue action, find – however momentarily distasteful it may be doing it – that it changes things for the better and end up saying 'I just wish I had done that sooner'.

If you find yourself putting things off in future try a moment's analysis and you may find that action more likely follows. Make this approach a habit and adopt a systematic approach:

- **Spot the areas needing action that you are in danger of failing to address.**
- **Ask yourself why you are turning away from something and check specifically that it is not simply to avoid what will (apparently) cause some personal discomfort.**

- Check that action is possible: do you know what to do? Do you have the skills to do it?
- Fill any information or skills gap, taking time so to do if necessary (this is usually time well spent, for example fire someone without checking out the employment legislation situation and you may make a small hole very deep).
- Schedule action into your list of 'things to do', giving it its true priority and having worked out what you have to gain (after all you deserve some motivation if you are going to choose to be uncomfortable).
- Take the action and take note: if it solves the problem, generates the opportunity – or whatever – learn from it for next time.

Make this a habit. Make entering the discomfort zone a catchphrase. This approach is the antidote to things going by default. It needs some resolve, but surely you have that. Here is truly a technique which, simply by overriding an undesirable element of human nature, provides a simple, sure way to increase your effectiveness and enhance the results you achieve; as a traditional proverb puts it: If you want to do something, you find a way. If you don't want to do anything, you find an excuse.

Handling personal interruptions

Organisations would be nothing without people. This is a pity in some ways, as you would otherwise certainly have a great deal more time. You cannot remove other people, but you can make attempts to control their unscheduled disruption of your work. Consider the effect first. Imagine someone sticks their head into your office and says, in those immortal words: 'Do you have a minute?' You may not know what it is about, but of one thing you can usually be absolutely certain: it will not take only a minute!

Interruptions may take any amount of time; you could find half the day disappearing on an unscheduled meeting. Now continue to imagine, let us say, that the visitor interrupts and takes up 15 minutes of your time. How long does that interruption last? Not 15 minutes, but just a little more as you have to get yourself back into whatever work was interrupted and this may take a little time, and possibly still more time to get up to the peak of performance that you were working at previously. This effect is worth bearing in mind or you can be apt to underestimate the impact of interruptions. Time logs often show a significant loss of time in this way, as much as 25 per cent of total working time sometimes being affected.

Of course, some interruptions are in themselves useful. You want to have the discussions they involve, but not at that moment; on the other hand some are a complete waste of time. So how do you minimise them? There are essentially five responses:

1. **Refuse them.** Simple; you just say 'no' and send the person away. Sometimes it is that easy, it was not an important matter, it can be sorted without your help and does not crop up again. Alternatively, the person will contact you again at another time. Of course, it is more difficult if it is your boss rather than a colleague, but you can acquire a mutual respect for each other's time in a working relationship. Then again, sometimes this route is simply not possible, whatever it is is simply too important and should take precedence, as with an unscheduled customer visit perhaps.
2. **Postpone them.** Say you cannot pause right now, but offer to fix a time for a discussion – or suggest one convenient to you – this still appears helpful and means you can choose when to pause. What is more, it is a technique that will make some interrupters go away with the response that it 'doesn't really matter'. Try this, you might be surprised how many never return.

3. **Minimise them.** Here you agree to pause, but you put a time limit on it – 'I can let you have 10 minutes.' If you do this, always stick to the time. In fact, by being disciplined in this way, you can create a reputation about your attitude to time and command respect, and this too will reduce interruptions a little.

4. **Prevent them.** In this case you need to instigate a system that provides some time guaranteed free of interruptions. You can plan and work this with a secretary, booking time for a job and treating it like an important meeting. But it can be simpler than that, and I know of cases where, even in an open plan office, people have agreed to respect a sign saying 'DO NOT DISTURB.' There is one proviso here: do not overuse this system. If you are never available, you will still finally get interruptions, or things you want to hear about will pass you by and something may go wrong as a result.

5. **Be somewhere else.** You may have the kind of job where you can choose where you work. People find a variety of, sometimes strange, places to repair to for a while to get the peace and quiet that improves productivity so much on some kinds of task. For example:
   – spending the first two hours of the day finishing that report at home before you come into the office;
   – visiting the public library reading room, a minute or two's walk from the office;
   – a nearby park (not with papers on a windy day);
   – for those who travel on business and sometimes have to stay in hotels, actually planning to take work along and stay on till checkout time rather than leaving first thing in the morning.

Some work on this book was carried out in a hotel in Singapore (when a training course was postponed). The only interruption during the entire time was the arrival of the next cold drink, but it was only possible because I never travel without having some work with me for such occasions – a good habit, I think, especially with work on a book of this particular title! Some ideas to reduce the number of drop-in visitors appear below.

Action to reduce the number of drop-in visitors

Some you want to see, some you do not, and many can be a complete waste of time. So, unless they are really useful or important (or a prime link in the grapevine) try some of the following to put them off:

- Insist on appointments whenever possible.
- Establish and publish 'do not disturb' times.
- Acknowledge them, but arrange another time to see them.
- Remember, it is easier not to start some discussions than to get out of them quickly (especially ones starting: 'I wonder if you could help?' Possibly, but should you? Or is there another way or time to help?).
- Brief your PA and/or other staff both to cope with more and to be firm where necessary.
- Use effective communications to reduce queries.
- Decide what needs to be originated in writing (though inappropriate memo writing can also be time wasting) and inform others.

And for the really awkward/difficult:

- Do not invite them to sit down.
- Set a time limit.
- Indicate an ending ('One more thing, then I must get on... ').
- Initiate other action to make any drop-in unnecessary, including visiting them.

And, above all: say 'no', or even 'NO' more often. You can be firm without being (too) rude.

Handling telephone interruptions

Sometimes you want to be immediately accessible; on other
occasions you can get your PA to act as a buffer, taking calls in the
first instance and checking who is calling. Clear briefing can
rapidly establish those you will pause for, those you will call back
and those to forget.

If you take the call yourself you are at a considerable
advantage compared with facing the head round your office door:
the caller cannot see you, and there are many who do not regard
saying they are busy, in a meeting, just leaving the office or
similar statements as too much of a white lie. I even know
someone who plays the noise of voices on a dictating machine to
give callers the impression that a meeting really is going on! Just
like physical interruptions, you can aim to avoid, postpone or
minimise them, and additionally you may wish to devise special
responses to particular kinds of call.

For example, how many calls do you get from salespeople in a
week? Enough for it to be a distraction most would say. Some of
them are useful, some you already do business with and want to
maintain the contact. But others you need to get rid of quickly.
Most of us are reasonably polite, and we do not like to be rude to
people, but consider: only one minute spent on the telephone
just to be polite, assuming you spend this with only three
telesales people every week, is two-and-a-half hours in a year.
And to save this time you still do not need to be rude. Find out at
once what they are selling – then you can listen if you want –
otherwise a neat sentence really early on will get rid of them fast:
'Sorry, that would not be of interest and I am afraid I am too busy
to speak now. Goodbye.' Then put the phone down. You can
always suggest another time to call back if you think a word with
them would be useful. People know and understand, from their
own experience, that the phone can be intrusive and tend to be
more understanding of your not necessarily welcoming a call at a
particular moment. Use this fact and save time.

All matters of handling these kinds of people interruptions

require the normal people-handling skills: tact, diplomacy, but also suitable assertiveness. These need to be deployed in the right mix and to the appropriate degree. If you are seen as insensitive and assertive to the point of rudeness this may well be destructive of relationships. But if you effectively lie down and ask to be walked on, then it should be no surprise when you are treated like a doormat. The following text adds some suggestions for reducing call intrusion.

Action to reduce telephone interruptions

All sorts of calls can be problematical, some just because they interrupt, others because you do not want (or should not have to) deal with them anyway, still more because they last unnecessarily long or the person at the other end is a chatterbox. The following suggestions may help with some of the calls you wish to discourage, or prompt further ideas:

- Check the information on which the switchboard operator assigns calls, and rebrief if necessary.
- Brief your PA well if you have one.
- Ask a colleague to take calls for a period (you might swap time doing this).
- Create clear 'do not disturb' times.
- Use a voicemail system (though watch the negative side of this, for example the image presented to outsiders, especially customers).
- Specify to others when to call you ('Why not call me back between 2 and 3 o'clock?' 'Please ring before 10 o'clock, as I will be tied up later in the morning... ') whenever possible.
- Remember, delegation will direct calls to others on topics they will deal with in future.

- Give people the name of your personal assistant/ secretary or a colleague (many people, when told you are busy will simply call back, even if asked whether someone else can help. If you actually say: 'If I am not here then do talk to my secretary, I will make sure he/ she knows about it... ', or similar, their reluctance to talk to someone else declines).
- Be aware of the time-wasting nature of social chatter and aim to curtail it before it gets out of hand (too much wastes time; none, and the world would be a less interesting place).
- Set a time limit ('OK, tell me about it now, but will you keep it to 10 minutes as I have a visitor due soon.' People would much rather be set a limit than be cut off halfway through, so this need not seem rude).
- Indicate the end is near, by using words like 'Finally... ', or 'Before I go... ', to make it clear to a caller you, at least, intend to stop soon.
- Failing all else, be rude; or at least consider whether part of the problem may be that you are just too concerned to be polite (fitting in time when the phone rings can become a reflex: we say 'Sure...' rather as we answer 'Fine' when asked how we are, however we actually feel).

Very important is the resolve and tenacity that you put into establishing approaches here. Some people seem conspicuously more successful than others at avoiding interruptions; if so they doubtless work at it. Precedents are easily set, for good or ill. There is a great deal to be gained by getting things right in this area and that includes ensuring you are seen in the right kind of way.

That said, there are other kinds of interruption and these too should be minimised. Bearing in mind (again) the cumulative impact of time savings, a few examples follow to conclude this chapter.

Save time getting through

I can never quite come to terms with this one. It always seems unbelievable how much time is wasted dialling, redialling and holding on the telephone, much of it these days listening to music and messages clearly designed to prompt insanity. What does make a real difference is a modern telephone. This is a form of digital technology I really warm to. They are not so complicated that they put you off and there are specific features that are real time savers. For example:

- **If you have the ability to store all the common numbers you use this will save you having to dial them; a couple of digits and the phone does the rest.**
- **Many will also redial (for example, if the chosen number is busy first time) and some will go on and on dialling automatically until they get through.**
- **A loudspeaker means that if you have to hold on (listening to the music) then your hands are free and work can continue.**

This is another, perhaps seemingly small, point that can make such a difference to your time. And each time you discover one the time saving adds up just a little more.

Make messages accurate

Without a doubt, a vast amount of time must be wasted in offices around the world because of inaccurate or incomplete messages. Time is wasted:

- **wondering what things are about;**
- **with things said once being repeated;**
- **with things having to be repeated or rephrased because of errors or breakdowns in communication.**

There are bound to be times when you are away from the office, and even if such absences are brief or infrequent, a good message system will save you time and prevent possible misunderstandings, which can have other effects.

The information you want may not be exactly that on commercial stationery forms. You need a message form that is designed for you. In this way, it acts as a checklist for those around the office as to the information you want noted. Small differences here are important. For example, a section for ACTION TAKEN as well as ACTION REQUIRED tells you exactly how far a conversation proceeded and allows follow-up without repetition.

I believe such forms should be in a style that declares their importance – after all, one lost message may change history (or at least cause major corporate or personal inconvenience). You must decide what suits. Maybe an A4 size page is best (it means it can be clipped together with other papers to make a neat file as well as being more visible). Maybe it should be on coloured paper so that it stands out amongst other office paperwork.

All this helps. So too does clear briefing as to what should be dealt with, passed on, how quickly and in what circumstances. For example, do you want everything sent on to a conference you attend for a couple of days, or only certain things? What about people – who is told where you are and who not? And so on.

It is a waste of everyone's time if you pass messages back to the office or leave dealing with them till your return. So, decide what you want to know, how messages should be taken and when, where and how they should be passed on. It is one more small thing that adds a little more to good time utilisation.

E-mail

This style of communication has rapidly become a major part of the variety of ways in which we all communicate. It is a major improvement. And if that makes you snort in anguish then you are not alone. Of course, e-mail is useful, but many abuse the system. It is so easy to send a copy to everyone in sight (or rather out of sight) so that people are returning to their desks and finding, even after a brief absence, that a veritable avalanche of e-mails awaits. Some are likely to be as necessary as any letter, memo or fax, but they take some sorting. Mix in some spam and the sorting becomes even more substantial.

Everyone can benefit from everyone else's discipline in this area. Keep the volume under control and all benefit. A routine is necessary too; if you check your messages every five minutes, just in case you have received something interesting, any time advantage of e-mail quickly evaporates. The effects of all this are many and various. Sending a whole file down a special telephone line in a moment may well save time, but other impacts, as with any technologically led change, may not be quite as we originally anticipated. Given the ubiquitous nature of e-mails, further information on their use appears at the end of this chapter.

On the move

Whatever travel means in your business life, whether you travel near or far or do so regularly, occasionally or often, it takes time. Some of that time can easily be wasted. Here we look at the essentials of time-efficient travel: first, whether to travel or not. What are the alternatives? You might consider:

- *Having people come to you.* **This may be possible – you may only have to suggest it or it may even be worth footing the bill, providing an overnight hotel stay; this will cost no more than you travelling in the reverse direction, and saves you time.**
- *Sending someone else.* **Yes, even to that attractively located conference, delegation must always be considered and is commented on elsewhere.**

- *Telephoning.* Some things really can be dealt with pretty simply and you do not need to be face to face, or an initial telephone contact gets something under way and a visit can come later when the project is less tentative and time spent on it more worthwhile. Note: mobile telephones – these seem to become more sophisticated as you watch, and it will doubtless only be a matter of time before one gadget strapped to your wrist will act as telephone, fax, generate e-mail and close the curtains in your living room while you sit in a restaurant on the other side of the world. Of course, mobile phones are invaluable for keeping in touch. They still need to be used carefully. Lengthy message-taking procedures when you are between phones may not facilitate good communication, and sometimes returning calls is delayed because some people are reluctant to call a mobile telephone because the cost is high. It is now possible to telephone someone thinking they are down the road from you and find your telephone bill reflects the fact that they were in Hong Kong. Some care is necessary still, perhaps, but, wherever you may be, mobile phones can minimise further travel.
- *Writing* (in whatever form – letter or e-mail). The same applies here as for the telephone, though the two forms of communication are different, one producing a written record. Remember, both may not generate such immediate or accurate understanding as a meeting.
- *Using technology.* For those able to afford it, modern telecommunications offer increasingly sophisticated possibilities, including telephone and videoconferencing where you can be linked electronically to a group of people all able to converse and even see each other.

So, before you call the travel agent, think for a moment. Of course some things can genuinely only be dealt with face to face and some journeys are essential – but not all. That said, when the journey is genuinely necessary, there are other considerations for those with an eye on maximising the effectiveness of their time, not least timing. If you must go, consider the logistics:

- *Plan every trip.* Consider priorities, timing and how an absence fits in with other things.
- *Consider cost.* Different routes or ways of travel (train or plane, class of ticket) may affect not just cost but time – sometimes time saved may make it worth paying more.
- *Location.* What is the best place to meet, for example halfway between your location and that of whoever you are meeting?
- *What to take.* For example flying with no check-in baggage saves time, taking a computer may improve your productivity (see below).

With a journey organised, the next thing to consider is using travel time constructively. Certain tasks lend themselves to being done on the move. Here are some things that you can do:

- *Reading.* It is useful to catch up with all sorts of material, and easy to do as you go along; even a short journey may get a report or other document out of the way.
- *Writing.* This needs better conditions, but a good deal can be done (and dictating too, if you do not mind those around you hearing if you are on a plane, say – better for the car or taxi where there is some privacy).
- *Computer work*, which includes word processing. With modern equipment, you quickly get into the habit of doing this kind of work on the move and mentally pushing the surroundings into the background.
- *Discussion.* This is clearly only for when you travel with colleagues. If you do, there is no reason why you cannot schedule a proper meeting complete with agenda.
- *Telephoning.* Mobile phones allow you do a variety of things (see above).

- *Thinking.* This is particularly useful. You may need no papers, no equipment, only the intention and the plan to do so. I keep in my diary a list of 'thinking things', longer-term issues, specifically needing no papers, so that I can turn this up when suitable moments occur.

Match tasks to the particular journey. You can type more easily on a plane. On a train and in a car other things may be better suited. Hotel rooms, airport lounges and more all provide opportunities. It is worth some thought and the amount you can get done, even in adverse circumstances, may surprise you. Indeed, adverse circumstances can be an especially good opportunity: if you are marooned in an airport by fog, will you have the appropriate things with you?

Do not waste time contacting your office every five minutes while you are away to do no more than say 'Is everything OK?' That wastes your time and that of others. On the other hand do make it clear what you must be told about, and do not forget the basics:

- **Leave a note of all your contact details.**
- **Advise when you can be contacted and when not.**
- **Advise of any changes to your arrangements as you go along.**
- **Give an idea in advance of the workload you will bring back for others and the urgency of such tasks.**
- **Plan for emergencies. For example, leave copies of your passport, credit cards and such in the office – any disaster can then be coped with by a single phone call (but check your insurance too before you go!).**

This is less an area of time saving than of making sure that time is not wasted because of lack of such details. Think also of anything that can more easily be done back at the office while you are away (even such things as spring cleaning it).

Although the areas of potential time saving are mounting up as this review progresses, and that is in itself useful, it must always be kept in mind why the time is needed. To do the tasks the job demands is too simplistic a way of putting this as, in most if not all jobs, some things are more important than others. In the next chapter we turn specifically to priorities – the first things first principle.

Thinking about e-mail

E-mail, or rather unthinking use of it, can waste large amounts of time. What follows are some thoughts prompted by this fact – it is not designed to be 'everything you need to know about using e-mail'.

First consider the level of formality involved. E-mail is usually much less formal than writing a letter. But having said this, the level of formality must be selected wisely. There are those to whom you may write very informally (incorporating minimal punctuation and as many abbreviations and grammatical shortcuts as you wish) as long as your meaning is clear. People replying to e-mails to do no more than check exactly what was meant must waste untold hours. But others (customers, senior colleagues) may resent this or think worse of you for it. Sometimes an e-mail must be as well-written as any important letter. It is safest to adopt a fairly formal style, and certainly a clear one, and err on the side of more rather than less formality if you are unsure. You have been warned! Proofreading is as important here as with many other documents; so too may be the use of the spellchecker.

Note: Computer viruses can arrive by e-mail, so don't consider it a waste of time to keep all antivirus software up to date and to use it correctly and regularly – failure to protect a system can result in big problems and may really teach you something about unproductive time. Similarly, personal use of the organisation's e-mail can waste time and have legal and disciplinary implications.

Some basic guidelines

As has been said, e-mails can be more informal than letters but certain standards with regard to style and content are sensible (again, some organisations set guidelines). Given the volume of e-mails people receive, you are competing for attention and must compose e-mails that are effective. An e-mail should be:

- **brief – use plain words;**
- **direct – clear presentation, no ambiguity;**
- **logical – with a clear structure.**

Whether e-mails are being sent internally or externally, as a substitute for a letter or not, it is important to ensure these rules are observed. A clear subject heading will make its purpose apparent and it may also be helpful to flag any (real!) urgency and say whether and when a reply is sought. Remember that e-mail can, like any communication, have many intentions – to inform, persuade, etc – and may thus need as much thought to compose as any other document.

Before sending an e-mail, consider the following to ensure that it is presented effectively:

1. What is the **objective** or **purpose** of the e-mail? Do you know what you are trying to achieve? Is the e-mail a request for information? Are you circulating standard information? If the e-mail is a quick response to a query, make sure that what you say is correct. If you are unsure, explain that this is an acknowledgement of receipt, and that you will come back to the sender as soon as you can. If you do not know what the objective is, think carefully before sending your communication.
2. What is the **background** to the issue? Is the reason for sending the e-mail something that is to do with a problem in a project? Is there an explanation, excuse or apology

required? Is it to elicit more information or to provide detailed answers to a query? For an e-mail to be clearly understood, there must be a reason behind it. If you don't know, check before clicking send.

3. Who is the intended **recipient**? Will it reach them direct, or will it be read by another person? E-mail in-boxes are not necessarily seen only by the person named in the e-mail address. It is possible that colleagues have access to a person's mailbox, for example when someone is sick or on holiday. It is important to bear this in mind when writing a message in case it may cause problems.

4. What **style** are you using? How is it being presented? Is the style really informal? Are you replying to a message that was half-encrypted with lots of missing capital letters, text-message style shortened words and emoticons, etc? If so, that is fine. But think carefully about what impression the style of the e-mail gives to someone who is opening a communication from you for the first time.

5. What is the **content**? What is the e-mail saying and is it being clearly communicated without any vagueness and ambiguity? If the e-mail covers complex matters, it may be better to explain that a document follows. E-mails are usually intended to be read and understood quickly, so the content should reflect this.

6. Is there a **conclusion**, recommendation or response required? If so, is this obvious? It may be clearest to place any request for action at the end of the e-mail. Also by saying something like 'It would be helpful if you could bring this information with you when we meet at 4pm', you will give the recipient a clear message that they have until 4 pm to complete the task. Finishing off an e-mail with a direct instruction, or repeating the purpose of the message, will leave the reader in no doubt about what your intention is.

7. What (if any) **attachments** are being sent? Specify any attachments clearly. If a device is used to squash

information together – such as zip files – it is always helpful to explain what system you use. If the attachments require certain software to open them, tell the recipient what is needed. This is particularly important where graphics and images are being sent. Some attachments can take ages to download,it is helpful to be specific.

Conveying yourself appropriately in an e-mail is important, because it is instant and non-retrievable. As with other written communication, there is no tone of voice, facial expression, posture, body language and gestures to augment your message. As e-mail is a rapid and concise form of communication, the detail matters (see below).

Best practice

These are some of the most important points of detail to remember when sending an e-mail:

- *Format.* Use an appropriate format or house style – this is often available as a template. Make sure it matches the style used in the company's letters and faxes and check what other aspects of layout are expected to conform.
- *Typography/font.* Most companies have a prescribed font and style but others can be chosen from the drop-down list in Outlook. The screenshot shows the font and size selected. You can also select the option to make bold, <u>underline</u> and *italicise* words, as you can in Word.
- *Subject.* Writer reference, case number or project name – this is just a polite way of ensuring that the recipient can save time by reading what the e-mail refers to. If you are sending an e-mail to someone about a particular matter, it is helpful if they understand immediately what the message is about.

- *Salutation.* Are you on first-name terms with the recipient? Do you need to write in a more formal style because you have not exchanged correspondence before? Do you know the name of the person to whom you are writing or would it be an impersonal salutation?
- *Punctuation.* Beware of ambiguity. A missing comma or no full stop can often cause confusion. It may be a lot quicker to lose capitals and miss out dots and dashes but if the reader is left puzzled by the meaning, you are less likely to get a useful exchange of information.
- *Line length.* Short sentences and line length make for easier reading on-screen. This is explained in more detail further on. Do not use complex sentences or syntax. Short and sweet is best.
- *Paragraphing.* Options are available from the drop-down list, including headings, bulleted and numbered lists. Paragraphing should be used where there is a change of topic or subject, so that the reader is aware that a new point is being introduced.
- Consistency. If the e-mail contains lists, take care. It is extremely irritating if the numbering changes in style or is inconsistent. If you are making several points, stick to a), b), c) or i, ii, iii or whatever style or format you prefer.
- *Valediction.* Unlike a formal letter you don't have to sign off 'yours faithfully' or 'yours sincerely', however in some cases it may be appropriate to end with an informal send off. Many people use 'kind regards', 'many thanks' and 'best wishes' or more impersonally, 'yours'.
- *Auto signature.* With e-mails it is possible to set up an auto signature as a default, which appears at the foot of each message you send. This includes your name and title as well as the details of the company you represent (such as address, switchboard number, fax and web address).

- **Attachment.** As mentioned before, these should be clearly described and mentioned in the text. If they are in different format, such as PDF files, it is a good idea to ensure beforehand that the recipient's computer is able to receive these files in readable form.

Security issues

There are a number of issues here and again, failure to address them can be costly in both time and money.

Time-wasting e-mails

This is an intractable problem, but some points are worth noting. Junk e-mails are a nuisance and can be time-consuming. E-mails received from reputable bodies sending legitimate commercial e-mail, as compared to 'illegal spammers', are within the law. The majority of illegal spam e-mails can be readily identified from the address and/or subject and immediately deleted without being opened.

Replying to illegal spam will often make things worse. The spammer will know that the e-mail address is valid, will continue to use it and will often circulate it to other spammers. Anti-spam filters have been mentioned and are incorporated in corporate IT systems as standard. They do not catch everything, but they certainly reduce the volume of spam reaching e-mail in-boxes.

It is possible to block some unwanted messages. There may be a number of reasons why e-mails need to be blocked from particular senders. Junk e-mails are just one of the main reasons; others include people with whom you no longer wish to correspond. By setting up barriers supplied with your e-mail package, specific e-mail addresses can be blocked. When a sender is blocked, their message will be diverted straight into the 'Deleted Items' folder. Do not forget to empty this folder regularly, otherwise it can become clogged with unwanted messages. You can easily remove a sender from the 'blocked senders' list by selecting the address and clicking the 'remove' button.

Beware of opening messages from unidentifiable sources, particularly with attachments. These can contain viruses or micro-programs that can access your information and send it to others.

Digital Signatures and other security devices

Several other things should be noted with regard to security:

- Digital IDs are being used more widely as an increasing number of people send information via e-mail. By using digital IDs or signatures you can ensure that no one is pretending to be you by sending false or misleading information under your name. Digital IDs in Outlook Express can prove your identity in electronic transactions, rather like producing your driving licence when you need to prove your identity. They can be used to encrypt (code) e-mails to keep the wrong people from reading them. Digital IDs are obtained from independent certification authorities whose websites contain a form which, when completed, contains your personal details, and instructions on installing the digital ID. This is used to identify e-mails and ensure security of your messages.
- Encryption is a special way to send sensitive information by e-mail. It is a form of electronic code. One code is used to encrypt the message and another code is used to decrypt it. One key is private, and the other is public. The public key is passed to whoever needs to use it, whether they are sending the message (in which case they would use it for encryption) or if they are receiving the message (in which case they would use it to decrypt the message).

- Records – some e-mail systems allow a note to be shown when an e-mail has been sent, received, opened and read by the recipient. This can be important in some time-critical instances, such as in finance, banking, law and property.

For all its advantages, e-mail needs careful use, not least in terms of time implications.

5

First things first

It may be a little late to be stating absolute fundamentals, but there is one fact upon which an individual's approach to time management must be based. This is simply that none of us can do more than one thing at a time. No one – ever. It is no use quibbling. Yes, of course there may be some overlap, but that is not the same thing at all. Like the 24-hour day, we are all stuck with this fact, and the fact is that what we do (and do not do, or spend less time on) is ultimately a crucial measure of success.

Time management is certainly about using methods that will increase the amount of real effective time available to you, but it is also about ordering the work within that time to produce a focus on the right things. As such, it is about priorities as much as it is about anything else. This chapter addresses a number of issues under this heading, and aims to give you some helpful ideas. Long term, however, one of the things that really separates the time-efficient from others is their ability to decide on their priorities easily and accurately. That is not something anyone gets 100 per cent correct, and is perhaps something that only comes with experience, but it is worth working towards.

Pareto's law

Before you can work effectively in deciding priorities, you have to come to grips with their importance. This sounds self-explanatory no doubt, and of course you may say some things are obviously more important than others. But it is very easy to underestimate just how much this concept influences what you need to do, indeed just how much it influences your inherent effectiveness. Pareto's law, named after the Italian economist Vilfredo Pareto, is now universally known as the 80/20 rule. It links cause and effect in a ratio and, although this is not represented absolutely accurately in real life, an approximate 80/20 ratio is found in many business activities, sometimes with considerable precision. This means that, for instance, 20 per cent of a company's customers are likely to produce 80 per cent of its revenue; 20 per cent of factory errors are likely to cause 80 per cent of quality rejects.

And it applies specifically in terms of the issues reviewed here also: 20 per cent of meeting time results in about 80 per cent of decisions made; 20 per cent of items to read that pass across your desk produce 80 per cent of the information you need in your work.

And, most important of all, 20 per cent of your work time probably contributes around 80 per cent of what is necessary to success in your job. So, it is enormously important to reflect this in the way you operate so that attention is focused on those key issues that have this dramatic effect.

You may not be able to readily identify exactly which of your tasks have this effect. Some things will be clear, others you may need to think about. Have a look at your job description, at your time log too and make yourself think through and decide just what it is about what you do that has the greatest effect. It may not always be obvious for all sorts of reasons. You may take some key things for granted. For instance, forgetting, once they have become a routine, how important they are. Certainly, you are unlikely to find a direct relationship between such a list of key issues and the things your time log shows you spending the most time upon.

Just this simple review may prompt you to make some changes to your work pattern. Clear objectives and a clear job specification, together with a clear idea of which tasks influence what results and which are key in 80/20 terms, are the only rational bases for deciding priorities. Give yourself these bases and you will be better equipped to work effectively both in terms of time spent on key issues, and in terms of reducing or eliminating corresponding minor matters. But it is curiously difficult at one level to decide certain priorities. If we ask why, it brings us to the vexed question of the urgent versus the important. The urgent and the important are different in nature yet both generate pressure to deal with them 'before anything else'. It may help to think here of four categories:

1. urgent and important;
2. urgent but not important;
3. important but not urgent;
4. neither urgent nor important (but still necessary).

Overall, the key is to think first and make considered decisions before letting particular circumstances push you into doing anything, or trying to do everything, first. Things that need actioning fast you must then either do, or delegate, at once; things that can wait should not just be put to one side, but should be planned or scheduled so that they get the time they deserve and then, in turn, get completed as appropriate.

This may seem difficult. It is difficult. But the difficulty is, at least in part, psychological. We do know what is most in need of action, certainly with hindsight, yet somehow the pressures of circumstances combine to give some things an 'unfair' advantage and we allow this to influence the decision. This is a prime area where resolve is more important than technique, and where there are no magic formulae. Making the right judgements in a considered way must become a habit if you are to remain organised in the face of such pressures. That said, there are other ways of focusing attention and time on priorities and we look next at some examples. First, what useful approach can you take to the varied bits and pieces you have to deal with?

Make the miscellaneous a priority

Let me rephrase that heading: make the miscellaneous a priority occasionally. Nothing is perfect and it is inevitable that as you plan and sort and spend most time on priorities, some of the small miscellaneous tasks mount up. If this is what happens – and for many people it is – then it is no good ignoring it and pretending that it does not occur. Rather you need to recognise the situation and decide on a way of dealing with it.

The best way is simply to programme an occasional blitz on the bits and pieces. Not because the individual things to do in this category are vital, but because clearing any backlog of this sort will clear paper from your desk and systems. (Remember 80 per cent of the paper that crosses your desk is less important than the rest.) So, just occasionally clear a few minutes, or an hour if that is what it takes, and go through any outstanding bits and pieces. Write that name in your address book, answer that memo, phone back those people who you wish to keep in touch with but who have not qualified recently as priorities to contact, fill in that analysis form from accounts and all the other things you know tend to get left out and mount up.

Ideally, there should be no bits and pieces. If you operate truly effectively then these sorts of things will not be left out. Pigs might fly. If you are realistic then, like me, you will find this useful. Be sure it does not happen too often, but when it does, you can take some satisfaction from the fact that a session to 'blitz the bits' clears the decks and puts you back on top of things, making you more able to deal with the key tasks without nagging distractions.

Schedule – backwards

Some tasks are straightforward. They consist essentially of one thing and all that matters is deciding when to complete them and getting them done. But many tasks are made up of a number of stages that may be different things you do yourself or with other people. In addition, some stages may be conducted in different locations and the whole process may take days, weeks or months. All of which makes it important to schedule such multi-stage things in the right way if all priority tasks are to be completed on time. What can happen is that you take on a project and begin by believing it is straightforward. Consider an example: you are to produce some sort of newsletter. Let us say it is in four stages:

1. deciding the content;
2. writing it;
3. designing it;
4. printing it.

You complete stage one and stage two, but at this point find it has taken somewhat longer than you thought. You hasten into stage three but halfway through it becomes clear that the complete job will not be finished on time. At that point, it may be possible to speed things up, but other priorities could suffer, or the only way to hit the deadline might then be to use additional help, spend additional money or both. What needs to be done is to approach scheduling from the far end of the cycle:

- **Start with the deadline.**
- **Estimate the time of each stage.**
- **Make sure that the total job fits into the total time available.**

- **Allow sufficient time for contingencies. Things cannot always be expected to go exactly according to plan.**
- **Look at the thing in isolation, see how it will fit in with or affect other current projects and responsibilities.**

It may be that you need to adjust the way stages work to fit with other matters that are in progress. For example, perhaps a certain stage can be delegated so that this is ready for you to pick up and take it through to the end. A number of options may be possible early on, whereas once you are part way through, the options decline in number and the likelihood of other things being affected increases. All that is necessary here is that sufficient planning time precedes the project, and that in thinking it through you see the overall picture rather than judging whatever it is as a whole and oversimplifying it by just saying 'No problem'.

Be honest about deadlines

You must have heard the cry: 'If I had wanted it tomorrow I would have asked for it tomorrow.' The biggest problem about deadlines is their urgency – so many things seem to be wanted yesterday (sometimes because of someone's bad planning) that if you are not careful you spend your life running to keep up. As the Red Queen told Alice: '... here you see it takes all the running you can do to stay in the same place. If you want to get somewhere else, you must run twice as fast as that.'

Deadlines must therefore be realistic, which was the burden of the point made in the previous section. Give yourself sufficient time, build in some contingency plans, and then you can deal with the thing properly and still be able to hit the deadline on time. Fine – or is it? There is another common complication to deadlines: people are dishonest about them. In some ways this is understandable – there may be a great deal hanging on a deadline being hit, and not only in terms of results but also of reputations. So, what happens is that if something must be done by the end of the month, it is requested for the 25th 'to be on the safe side'. But this practice, and the people who do it, become known around an office and so the recipient of the deadline decides that a week later is fine. If several people are involved then the misjudgements can get worse as things are passed on and, overall, the chances of missing the date increase. It is ironic, but what starts out as a genuine attempt to ensure a deadline is met, ends up actually making it less likely that it will be.

The moral is clear. In any group with which you are associated, try to make sure the situation about deadlines is clear and open, and that everyone approaches the situation similarly. If something needs completing on the 10th of the month, say so. If some contingency is sensible, again say so: 'This has to be with the client on the 10th, let's aim to have it ready two days ahead of this to give time for a last check and make sure there is no chance of our failing to keep our promise to them.' This not only makes it more certain that the deadline involved will be hit, in part because people like this approach and commit to it more certainly, but also prevents other things being at risk because time is being spent chasing a deadline that is not, in fact, the real one. There is sufficient pressure in most offices without compounding the problem artificially.

While many, many things have to be completed by a deadline (including writing this book), there are some where exactly how they are done affects how long they take. With these, a review of methodology can pay dividends in saving time; with others such a review may allow the decision that they do not need actioning at all. And there may be more of these than you think. However, consider first those things that must be done but might be done differently from the way they are undertaken today.

Review task methodology

Another useful way to ensure you have adequate time for priority tasks is to review how exactly they, and other tasks too for that matter, are undertaken. Clearly, how you do something – the methodology – affects how long it takes. Because of this, there is sense in reviewing working methods on particular tasks and perhaps in doing so regularly. I am not suggesting that you stop all other work and spend time only on an examination of how things are done, but that you set yourself the job of reviewing a series of things over a period of time to search for worthwhile improvements.

Consider the example of my writing work again. The first book I wrote I drafted in longhand, my secretary typed it on a typewriter, and a long process of editing and retyping began. Since then I have typed my own material and the process has both changed and simplified. I still have to decide what to write (I would not want the publisher believing it was too easy!) but the whole process takes much less time and even though I have had to learn to type – not perfectly – the overall time saving is worthwhile and, of course, there are other advantages. For example, I can type on the move, on a journey for instance, and this saves still more time. Obviously, the changes that might be made to any task will depend on the nature of it, but all sorts of things can be worthwhile, for example:

- **Systematising a task that was previously more random or circuitous.**
- **Changing actual methods (as with my example above).**
- **Working with someone else (for example, again in my work, I do a little copywriting and brochure design, and always check the copy with one of my associates; another view focuses the process much more certainly and quickly than just thinking long and hard about it alone).**
- **Lower standards. One method may achieve perfection, another – faster – one may achieve a lesser, but perfectly acceptable, result and sometimes save money.**
- **Subcontract. In other words pay an external supplier to do something that they can do quicker, and sometimes cheaper and better, than you.**

Again, such a list could go on and you may be able to think of routes to action that suit your particular job and work best for you. However, the principle of checking to see if there is a better way of doing something is sound. This needs active review and an open mind. Anything you can think of to prompt the process may be worth considering. Maybe if you select certain tasks and swap them with a colleague this will bring a fresh mind to bear and prompt new thinking about methodology; you do something for them and they for you. However it happens, make it happen, for there is never only one right way of doing anything for ever, and improved methodology can be a great time saver.

Eliminate the unnecessary

Most people will deny, if asked, that they spend time doing things that are unnecessary; after all it seems absurd. But it does happen. And it happens for all sorts of reasons. Consider a few examples:

- *Habit.* You have always attended a monthly meeting, read a regularly circulated report, checked certain information, filed certain items and kept in touch with certain people. And it is easy for things to run on, repeating automatically without thought and for such things to take up time unnecessarily.
- *Insurance.* You do things for protective reasons. In case something goes wrong, in case someone asks why, in case... what? Sometimes the reason is not clear, there is just a feeling that it is safer to do something than not. Filing and documenting things are examples of this.
- *Avoidance.* The real reason for something to be done has long disappeared, but continuing to do it means you have no time – and excuse – to take on or try out something new and perhaps risky. Be honest, have you really never put off doing something new?

- *Expectation.* You do things not because of their real worth, but because it is, or you feel it is, expected of you. In a team environment you do not want to let others down, though you will let things down more by ignoring priorities.
- *Appearances.* You do things because they are 'good things' to be involved with, perhaps politically, and every organisation has some politics. Your position and people's perception of you around the organisation are important, but you must not overdo this kind of involvement, not least because it can become self-defeating, being seen as the ego trip of someone who has nothing better to do.

All of these and more may occur and, make no mistake, there are no doubt valid reasons under each heading – you really do need to attend some meetings simply to demonstrate commitment and this is a tangible and priority result. But... but, this is an area you need to be quite tough about. Are there any things you are doing that you can stop doing without affecting the results significantly? For most people an honest appraisal shows the answer to be 'yes', so review it immediately if you have not done so for a while, and regularly afterwards to ensure that unnecessary tasks are not creeping in again.

How is this done? Very simply (it is something consultants like me spend a lot of time doing with their clients), you ask why? Why is something being done? And if the answer is because that is the way it is, that is the system, or, worst of all, that is the way it has always been done, then ask again. If you cannot really find a better reason then the task may well be a candidate for elimination. Failing that, maybe you can do it less often, in less detail or otherwise adjust the approach to save time and allow attention to be given to the priorities. This is another area that can start from the time log; it is not just what you are doing that matters, but the time it takes. If you are ruthless about this kind of questioning and honest about the answers then time may be saved in this way.

Danger – keep your distance

One particular kind of task may very sensibly be categorised as unnecessary, at least to you. Black holes, collapsed stars so massive and with such powerful gravity that they pull in everything and even light cannot escape from them, make the old expression about going down the plug hole seem pretty small beer. In most offices, there are corporate equivalents of this phenomenon, 'black hole jobs' that suck in all the time you can think of and more. Watch out for them and beware – just like real black holes, if you get too near there is no going back and an involvement means all your other plans have to be put on hold. What kind of jobs warrant this description? They include projects that:

- **involve a number of different, and complex, tasks;**
- **may be contentious;**
- **are impossible to complete and please everyone;**
- **may be ruinous of reputations;**
- **take up a quite disproportionate amount of time.**

They encompass a range of things from organising the company's twentieth-anniversary celebrations to moving the company to new offices. Such things have to be done (you may have such things in your job description, in which case it is a different matter), but they often call for 'volunteers'. This can mean the Managing Director suggests it, in public, in a way that makes refusal risky: 'It is only a suggestion, of course, but do bear in mind who's making it.' At this point, others heave sighs of relief and resolve not to get involved even in a tiny support role.

You will know, if you have any wits at all, the kind of tasks in your office that have these characteristics and you should, if you value your ability to keep on top of your other tasks, plan to be well away whenever there is a danger of you getting lumbered with one. Do not say you have not been warned.

Be confident of your priorities

The best time managers organise successfully to concentrate time and energy on their priorities and one reason they do so seems to be an ability to make prompt and firm decisions about what should be priorities. Others use up hours of valuable time not only deciding what should come first, but reviewing the decision again and again to double-check it. Of course, circumstances change and some ongoing review may be necessary but it does not help, as the saying has it, to keep digging up the plant to look at the roots to check if it is growing well. Similarly, the constant reassurance some people seem to seek in their decisions may just waste time and is also, in my view, a certain route to stress.

The decision process starts with review and analysis. Remembering that you can only do one thing at a time, you must be clear what the key factors on your list are and which are in fact most important, and constitute the real priorities. Having considered all sides of this thoroughly, you need to make a decision. There is no reason at that point to doubt that it is other than a good one.

And, in any case, no amount of further review will change the fact that you can do only one thing at a time, and however illogical, it is this that a long list of 'Things to do' sometimes prompts us to look to change. It does not matter whether the first thing to be done is followed on the list by 10 more or 100 more, something has to come first.

So, make the decision, stick to it, and get on with the task. The quicker you do that the sooner you will be able to move on down the list. Much is written about stress in the workplace (though not by me). Stress is a reaction to circumstances rather than the circumstances themselves. You should be able to say that you:

- **know your priorities;**
- **have made work planning decisions sensibly, based on reasonable and thorough consideration of all the facts;**

- are sure there is no more, for the moment, you can do to make things easier;
- know that as you proceed with the task you are going to do it effectively and that the methodology you will use makes sense.

This should then allow you to be comfortable about the process, and to reject any tendency to stress. Trying to work at something while worried that there may be greater priorities, knowing that a variety of other things are queuing up for attention but are as yet unsorted, and having any doubts about the way you are doing things is a sure recipe for stress. Keep calm by keeping organised and you will be better placed to maintain and increase your effectiveness.

Getting your priorities clear is not an area to be underestimated. Work at it. Look at your time log, analyse what you do and you may find with some initial horror that there are quite a number of things that you do that can be left undone (forever or for a moment) without causing any problem. You can then turn to looking creatively at how to use the time saved.

6

Controlling the paperwork

*You see things; and say 'Why?' But I dream
things that never were; and say 'Why not?'*

George Bernard Shaw

Let us start on a positive note. Paperwork need not overpower you. You can keep it under control, though you may not be able to eliminate it altogether. It is necessary, or certainly some of it is, and here we are 20 years after the IT experts began to talk about the 'paperless office' and there still seems to be as much as ever on my desk. Letters, memos, faxes, reports, forms, proposals, and more, all combine to create a steady stream of paperwork across your desk. If you are not reading things, you are writing them, and if you are not doing that you are processing things that involve paperwork. All this can take up a significant proportion of your working day. In time management terms the job is to:

- **eliminate it;**
- **minimise it;**
- **process what must be done promptly and efficiently.**

Here we consider a range of ideas, large and small, that can help you keep the paperwork under control. It is not exhaustive, no such review could be, but these ideas are an important way of thinking about how papers should be dealt with. Ultimately, because what constitutes the papers on any individual's desk is unique, we must all find our own solutions to this problem. The principles here, however, are selected to provide a suitable foundation for that basis. And as good a place as any to start is with some thoughts about minimising the volume of paper you deal with day to day.

Aim to minimise paperwork

Perhaps the first thing to ask in this area is simply: is all your paperwork really necessary? Let it be clear straight away, much of it will be. One such example, which this book has already recommended, is that your work/time plan be in writing. But some paperwork can be eliminated, and often all that is necessary is to pause for a second before you write something, and ask yourself whether what you are about to do is really necessary. Have a look at what is on your desk, see how much of it is not really necessary, think how much of it could achieve its aims in some other way. Yet, someone is sending all this to your desk and is presumably well intentioned in doing so. Perhaps much of what you create on paper is similarly regarded.

So, what do you do about it? The key alternative to written communication is the telephone; it is usually much quicker to lift the telephone than to write something, and, as not everything needs a written record, this is one of the surest ways of reducing paperwork.

It is also worth a note here about the now ubiquitous e-mail. It is not so much the sense of urgency this bestows on things that interests us here (though it is undeniably useful), it is the style. It seems that an altogether less formal style has developed for e-mail, one that is perfectly acceptable internally in a big company with a number of offices, and between external organisations, as a quick form of communication where brevity is essential. Brevity saves time, but it must be easily understood too. Print out and file e-mails where appropriate, and keep those listed in your computer manageable.

Two other points are worth a mention. In the interests of slowing the destruction of forests to make paper, as much as time, consider copies. It is one thing to write to someone, but it is the circulation of copies that feeds the proliferation of paperwork as much as anything. Think before you list half the company; who really needs a copy?

Can your document be standardised? There may be a number of routine communications that can be recorded in the word-processor – either whole letters or documents or separate paragraphs that can be used to put together something suitable. Here technology really does save time. But there is one very important caveat here. Never – never – use standard material if it is inappropriate. In the sales area, for example, I see many letters and proposals that shout 'standard' when they should be seen as an individual response. Further, any standard material should be double-checked to see that it is well written. Otherwise, by definition, something poor or, at worst, damaging may be sent out repeatedly. It can certainly save time but should not do so at the cost of an unacceptable reduction in quality.

Make a habit of brevity

Your written communication will be less time-consuming if it is not only brief but, choosing my words carefully, succinct and precise and, of course, clear (this is not the place for a treatise on making communications understandable, but communication should never be assumed to be easy. It is often the reverse, and misunderstandings must be responsible for a massive amount of wasted time as things are queried and clarified). This is worth a short (sic) paragraph here because I notice many people have a

curious reluctance to write short business letters. An example
makes the point: A writes to B prior to a meeting asking when his
flight arrives and whether he would like to be met at the airport.
So often the reply will be along the lines of:

> **Dear Mr A,**
> **Thank you for your kind letter of 24 July 2009 about my**
> **forthcoming visit to your offices next week on Thursday**
> **30 July. I am pleased to say that all my travel**
> **arrangements are now complete – you may remember I**
> **was having trouble with one of the connections – and I**
> **now have full details. I arrive on Flight 915 at 10.00 am.**
> **This should suit our lunch meeting well and not make**
> **any problem with the timing. With regard to your kind**
> **offer to meet me, perhaps I could say how grateful I**
> **would be for your assistance in this regard...**

And so on. If the two know each other even a little, surely there
can be nothing wrong with something that says:

> **Dear Mr A,**
> **It was good to hear from you. I arrive on Flight 915 at**
> **10.00 am on 30 July. It would be a great help to be met**
> **at the airport; I will look out for your driver. Many**
> **thanks, I look forward to seeing you soon...**

I know which I would prefer to receive: the second. The
information is clear, I do not have to wade through any
extraneous material, it saves me time, and may well be one-third
or one-quarter of the length of the first one. And it took less time
to write and send. I think it is still perfectly polite and I wish

more people adopted just this kind of approach. If it can be said in three lines then say it in three lines. Now consider the time saving of three-page memos reduced to one, reports of 10 pages instead of 20... but I promised this would be a short paragraph. Enough said; point made.

Minimal memos

The well-known memo makes up a major part of the paperwork in many offices. In the last section, I made a plea for brevity; here is a simple idea that can save even more time. Assume you receive a memo – a full page of some colleague's meanderings no doubt – and what it says is just: 'Can you attend a meeting of the planning committee at 3pm this coming Friday?' Assume that you can and are prepared to attend. Now all you need to do is photocopy the memo that came to you, write 'TO:' at the top and ring the name of the original sender, write 'FINE, SEE YOU THERE' at the bottom and sign it. If you really want to be rash with time, take an extra second and add a ring round your message to highlight it (a red pen does this nicely). Then send it back.

Excuse a touch of sarcasm here, but one so often sees people laboriously preparing typed and sometimes over-long memos when this kind of procedure will do very well; some companies have pre-printed sheets for their memos that are designed to take a reply. E-mail is helping this process; many e-mails are brief, and this developing style seems set to become a habit. Remember, however, the comments about the time-wasting tendencies of e-mail already made.

A final thought. In such circumstances you can always telephone, though consider who it is, how long they will chat and whether they would appreciate confirmation in writing for the record.

Minimise your paper handling

Here is an interesting experiment you can try (it will not take long and could end up saving you time). Select 10 or so items that come across your desk today, a mixture of letters, memos and documents, all of which demand some action on your part, and mark them all with a red spot in the top right-hand corner. Then simply deal with them as normal. And every time you touch them thereafter add another red spot to the top right-hand corner. As time passes you will then produce a count of how many times things go through your hands. For example, a letter arrives today and:

- **you read it;**
- **you decide not to deal with it immediately but put it with a job on which you intend to spend time in the afternoon;**
- **in the afternoon you make a start, work out what needs to be done but are interrupted;**
- **the letter joins a number of items that overrun the day and you pick it up again the following morning, and so it goes on.**

In this case we are imagining just a simple letter. In other cases, projects and processes span weeks or months; you can imagine the incidence of red spots. This is known as the 'measles test' and it can help you identify how your way of handling things affects the time that dealing with them takes. Sometimes the multiple 'spotting' is necessary, but other cases may well surprise you because you had no idea just how often some things cross your desk before they are resolved. The first step towards change is to know where change should be applied. The information gained in this way will be useful. Sometimes improvement is easy, for example the use of a Prompt File (see Chapter 3) will cure some 'spotting'. In other cases it may lead you to review your method of handling certain tasks. In any event, you should adopt the principle of trying to handle things the minimum number of times before they are resolved.

If you have a clear plan and a system for categorising your work then things should be dealt with immediately, or held for some reason and then dealt with. If this is applied rigorously, then the time taken up by papers being handled many times will be reduced. But again let us be realistic. Most jobs are not, in fact, made up of thousands of completely separate tasks, though it would perhaps be easier if they were. For a lot of people there are a great many links between different items and areas; indeed an element of some jobs involves creatively seeing links that can be turned into opportunities, and with the process of what is called synergy (or colloquially the $2 + 2 = 5$ effect). All of this may demand sufficient review of the situations represented by your paperwork for this opportunity process to be possible. So this rule, like some others, must not be applied slavishly. You need sufficient sight of some items to operate effectively and must be careful not to reduce paper handling in a way you feel does not suit or work well in your individual job.

I have no wish to create a straitjacket for readers with anything I suggest. However, the principle advocated here is sound and as a general rule being aware of how many times things go through your hands and trying to keep that number down makes good time-sense.

Do not let files and filing waste time

I once saw a cartoon that showed a picture of a world-weary-looking secretary standing by a manager's desk. She was holding a bundle of papers and the caption depicted her saying: 'Do you want this again – or shall I file it?' And there, in a nutshell, is the problem of filing. Too often it is used simply as a way of getting paper off the desk, and while there is some sort of system to suggest where papers go, there is no real thought about just what should be kept, or for how long, and it is this that wastes time. A frightening statistic emerging from a survey in one multinational giant showed that only 10 per cent of the papers put into filing were ever referred to again; this in an organisation proud of its efficiency – what hope for ordinary mortals?

This means that 90 per cent could have been destroyed, and the cost of 'keeping them at the right temperature in comfortable surroundings', as the survey called it, is enormous. The time wasted, our consideration here, is equally worrying. But some things do need to be filed, so you cannot throw the baby out with the bath water; you need a system.

By all means let a secretary design or help with the design of a system, but to achieve consistency you should always decide what goes where. Do the papers about that reorganisation go under R for reorganisation, O for organisation or office, E for efficiency drive, or B for boss's pet projects? There are often serious problems here, as anyone who has tried to locate a file, say, a year old, knows; few have memories that will hold this kind of detail forever. So, get the system right. It is difficult to generalise, you may need account files, project files or a dozen more; or all of these. It is usually better to have a number of categories, each A–Z, rather than one giant system that has to cope with everything. As you review potential filing material you only really have three options for action:

- **do not file it, throw it away;**
- **file it with no thought for how long it will stay there;**
- **file it with a clear indication of a destroy date (or at least a review date).**

Let me prompt you to think carefully about how much you need to keep things and then review some ways of keeping filing under control. Consider what is on or around your desk at present. How much of it could you throw away right now? Probably the answer is very little. But imagine those same papers in the future, how many of them will you need in six months, in a year, in two years? Here the honest answer will be fewer and getting even fewer as you go into the future. So why not throw more away? Think about where else things are held. If you need to check something in, say, a regular financial summary only once in three months, why even have a file on it if you know you can get it from the accountant in 30 seconds? Think about the things you hold 'just in case'. In your heart you probably know you are not at all bad at judging what will be required, yet you still keep too much. Trust your instincts, remember the old saying: if it looks like a duck and quacks, then it probably is a duck. If you are 99 per cent sure it is going to be rubbish very soon, you are probably right; after all, they are your papers. So throw them away.

But if you are wrong and need something you have thrown away, which may do more than waste time, consider some insurance. There are two systems that will provide this. First, batch filing – this is where filing is not done too early. Everything is put in simple A–Z order in a batch file and only filed after, say, a month (you pick the time). But before it is filed you look through it to see what you still want to keep. After even one month, you might be surprised how much you ditch. Second, the 'chronology' file – this system works by filing an extra copy of every letter and document produced for you in straight A–Z date order in something like a large lever arch file. This is kept for a fixed length of time, maybe a year in quarterly files to make it more manageable. Every time the fourth quarter file is full, the first quarter file is thrown away and you start a new quarter file with the current material. Either system or both may suit you. They let you be a lot more ruthless in throwing paper away, because on the odd occasion you are proved wrong you can find it in the back-up file.

Many systems benefit from a destroy system. This can be done by setting dates (perhaps in year batches) or even very simply by capacity. I have one file, kept in date order, which works by throwing something out of the drawer every time something new is added. The drawer is always just on full, and this corresponds well with how long the contents appear to remain useful and no one has to waste any time over it.

This area must be systemised on a basis that works for your office. If things are well ordered, if you can find what you want (and this is inherently easier if there is not so much in total to look through) and do not have to spend time constantly resorting the system to make room for more and more, then it will work well and you will run it and it will not run you. Order in the filing must save time.

Note: if your files are, even in part, in your computer, consider what printed versions you should have – *and take regular back-up files and store them separately.* I know you know this, but do you do it?

Keep papers neat

I like to think that I never lose things (well rarely!). But on the last two of those rare occasions, I discovered the lost papers caught under a paper clip hidden at the back of a batch of different correspondence. It is a small point perhaps, but you can waste some time hunting for papers and re-collating papers that have got out of order in this sort of way. Paper clips are not the best way to keep papers tidy. Beware – they do tend to trap other items and catch you unawares.

But papers must be kept tidy. Do not keep too much together (it becomes unmanageable), and worry in particular about files and papers that travel about with you both around and out of the office. Staple them, punch them or bind them rather than use paper clips, and experiment with whatever sort of files – and there are many different styles – suit you. I favour the sort that have a small top and bottom flap to hold things all round and elastic bands that snap across the corners. The more things you have to work on in parallel, the more your current papers need organising neatly.

If you only get one file out at a time and work on that until it is neatly replaced by something else, then it is less of a problem. If you are paid to keep many balls in the air at once, then it is vital. Time management is, in this respect, similar to juggling. If there are a lot of balls in the air and one is dropped, more tend to follow. The more you have on the go, the greater the disruption and waste of time if something becomes disorganised. Keep papers physically under control.

Computerise it – but carefully

It became one of the great 20th century myths that computers would transform office work, and make everything fast and efficient to action. But like other great promises ('Our cheque is in the post') it is not entirely to be trusted. Now, I have nothing against computers and there are things that one cannot now imagine working any other way, and yet... there are questions, certainly as far as efficiency and time utilisation are concerned, at desk level for the individual executive. There are examples of things now available that manifestly work well:

- **computerised databases that can be accessed on a desktop PC and dramatically reduce the time needed to sort through, analyse or communicate with those names on them;**
- **graphics programs that can turn a set of confusing figures into a graph and impart a key point in a moment;**
- **desktop publishing (DTP), which means documentation can be produced in-house at the touch of a button, removing the need to liaise with three separate outside suppliers;**
- **e-mail systems, which can allow easy, rapid communication with a branch office, say, or overseas contact, and allow you to peep into their files;**
- **computerised versions of things like drawing diagrams, analysing figures, interpreting statistics (and playing noughts and crosses!), which make their manual equivalents look positively quaint.**

You can probably think of many more. Some you will use and regard as routine, and many can save time. Yet, there are systems that for all their cleverness do not fit their role so well. Think of some of the systems you may be frustrated by as a customer, in the bank, insurance company or hotel. Consider a hotel account. They are, presumably, efficient for the hotel but many are very difficult to fathom without a degree in abbreviations. Customer service suffers. So there is another side to computers; you need expert help to set up many systems (and in some cases to operate them), there is a high capital cost though this is coming down, and they are all too readily used as an excuse for not doing things (if I had a small coin for every time I have heard someone in a travel agents say: 'Sorry, the computer is down', I could travel round the world free). Above all, they take time to set up and the equation of time must be carefully balanced to see what makes best sense.

There are things in this area that are great time savers. There are also pitfalls, costly in time, for the unwary. By all means use what you can, check out new things as they become available, but consider the alternatives as well and you may conclude some of them still hold good. If you can find that telephone number faster just by turning it up in a pocket notebook, why not do just that until something comes along that really is better for you?

Do not duplicate information unnecessarily

There is time expended in maintaining any information system. If the information is being recorded in identical or similar form in several different places, then the time is longer. This is worth checking, and there is a quick check you can run in a few moments. Rule up a matrix with information on one axis and places where it is kept on the other. If this produces columns of ticked boxes, then you may be holding information in too many places.

Such an analysis will quickly show the extent of any kind of duplication – and the sheer extent of the recording going on. If you then think about where information is most often sought, you may well find that only a minority of places originally listed are highlighted. This in turn poses questions about the other places where the information appears. How many of them can be scrapped or reduced? Time and neglect, or if you want to feel better about it, concentration on other matters, allow a proliferation of systems and information over time, sometimes far beyond what is really useful at present. Incidentally, another area to watch is computer information systems in which the technical ability to include extra information is often sufficient reason for it to be included. It is the use that is made of such sources that is important.

Do not proliferate information unnecessarily

Sometimes tasks seem important and then something happens that shows that this was not true at all, or perhaps not true any more. One thing that sometimes happens is that time is wasted because once something is originated then thinking about it ceases. An experience of mine will illustrate this. In one company where I did some work, I asked if they had certain information (sales analysis). At first, the answer was that they did not, then someone in the sales office said that they in fact sent such a breakdown to the Managing Director's office each month. The Managing Director denied all knowledge of this, but his secretary, overhearing the request, said she held a file of the information.

We checked and there it was. It arrived on her desk each month and she filed it. On tracking this back, we discovered that some two years previously the Managing Director had asked for this special analysis and a summary for that month had been produced. He had looked at it and put it in his secretary's filing tray, and she had opened a file for it. The sales office produced it again the next month, sent it to the MD's office, but his secretary filed it without showing it to him. This had then been repeated every month for two years! It took someone in the sales office several hours each month to complete the work to produce the figures, and, after the first time, it had all been a complete waste.

Such situations continue all too easily once the initial moment has passed. Just who was at fault? The sales office, the MD, the secretary? All three? It *just happened* they might say, but, more to the point, could it have been prevented? You should make a rule that whenever you are asked or need to provide any information to anyone (with copies to whoever else), you make a diary note to check at some time in the future – in 6 or 12 months perhaps – whether it is still necessary. Find out whether it still needs to be sent:

- **with the same frequency (would quarterly be as good as monthly?);**
- **to all the listed people;**
- **in as much detail (would some sort of summary do?).**

Any change that will save time is worthwhile and you may find that it is simply not necessary any more. Very few people will ask for information to stop coming to them, but if asked may well admit that they can happily do without it. Be aware of this sort of thing, or it is quite possible that all around your organisation things will be repeated unnecessarily.

Do not put it in writing

I felt for the course delegate who told me that a 20-page report he had been asked to prepare had been handed back by the manager to whom he presented it with a request for a verbal summary. While he had lavished care and attention on the report, he was unprepared for this and his spur of the moment presentation was not as fluent as he would have wished, the matter to which the report referred was dropped and the report was never read (it was no doubt filed rather than destroyed). He was naturally aggrieved and resented the incident – with some cause perhaps.

Certainly, management ought to consider the time-wasting consequences of its action, decisions and requests. What avoids something taking up time for you may land someone else with a great deal of extra work. If you are a manager, your responsibility for good time utilisation covers the team. It is little good being productive yourself if everyone else is tied up with all sorts of unnecessary tasks and paperwork. Jobs need to be done, action taken, consideration given and in many cases written instructions, guidelines or confirmation are not simply necessary, they are vital. But on other occasions that may well not be the case. The report referred to above should, in all likelihood, not have been requested. Certainly, the action, or lack of it, was decided upon without the detail documented in the report being looked at, and presumably the manager concerned felt he had enough information to make a valid decision. This kind of thing can often happen. Time may be wasted unless the instigator of such action thinks first and only specifies written details of something if it is really necessary. Similarly, those in receipt of such requests should not be afraid to ask, and check whether such exercises are really necessary. Whichever category you are in, and it may well be both, give it a thought. Of course, there are other considerations. If you just say 'Shan't' next time the Managing Director asks for a report, do not come crying to me if you are read the riot act. But in many circumstances, a check can and should be made (even with the MD) and less paper is put about as a result.

Write faster

Now 'Write faster' may seem in the same category of advice as maxims such as 'Save water, shower with a friend', and you may well ask what you are supposed to do – rush through things so that you write rubbish? No – the point concerns the quality of writing. Think of the last reasonably complicated document you had to write, a report perhaps. You had to think about what to say and how to say it, and design the structure and sequence in which the message was to be presented. All this might have taken some time; so too could have editing to get it right.

A systematic approach, one that decides the message first and considers exactly how to put it second, thus separating two tasks and making the whole thing less complicated, will not only help you write better – it will make you write more quickly. It is beyond our brief to go into the detail of this here (see *Effective Business Writing*, published by Kogan Page, in which I have written about this in some detail). Suffice to say that if you must regularly write then this is an area worth some investigation.

WPB – the most time-saving object in your office

Finally, in this section the nature of office paperwork is such that it is only right to end by returning to the simple premise of throwing things away. The WPB is, of course, the waste-paper basket. It helps efficiency and time if your desk and office are tidy, if what you need is neatly and accessibly placed – a place for everything and everything in its place – but not if such good order is submerged under sheer quantity of paper, most of it of a 'just in case' nature.

All sorts of things cross your desk: magazines, direct mail, items marked 'To read and circulate' and 'For information', copies of things that are of no real relevance to you and minutes of meetings that you wish had never taken place. Much of this causes you to pause for far too long, creating heaps and extra filing trays and bundles in your briefcase (things to read at home, for instance). It is better to deal with things early rather than later. When it has mounted up it is always going to be more difficult to get through, and an immediate decision will keep the volume down, for example:

- **If you are on a circulation list and do not want to look at something today, then add your name further down the list and pass it on; it will get back to you later when you may be less busy.**
- **At least check a magazine once, maybe you can tear out an article or two and throw the rest away.**
- **Consider very carefully whether the vast plethora of things that 'might be useful' are, in fact, ever likely to be; either file them or throw them away.**

All these kinds of thinking and action help, but most people are conservative and reluctant to throw things away. Unless you are very untypical, there will be things on and around your desk right now that could be thrown out. Have a look, and, as you look, do some throwing. Make a full WPB a target for the end of the day. Imagine it has a scale running down the inside to show how full it is. This scale could almost be graduated, not in volume, but in minutes saved. The paperless office may still be a way off; in the meantime, keeping what there is under control is certainly an important part of the time management process.

7

Working with other people

People seem to want to follow the beaten path
The difficulty is that the beaten path doesn't
seem to lead anywhere.

Charles M Mathias Jnr

You will encounter people of all sorts in business. Some you will
get on with, some you will not; some will help you, inform you,
or teach you; some will infuriate you; some you will work with,
getting things done that would not happen otherwise. But, male
or female, young or old, senior or junior – all will waste your
time. Some will do so intentionally, others unwittingly, but it will
happen.

What is more, because people interactions in business are
vital, there is no way of avoiding them, but you have to work with
people in a way that anticipates and minimises the disruptive
effect they can have on your time. Here we look at a range of
topics, useful in themselves, and as examples of the approach to
take, that help. Some will be most appropriate if you manage
other people, others are more generally applicable; all will save
you time.

Let us look at general people issues first. The intention here is to give the feel of a whole range of 'people issues' that can affect the utilisation of time either positively or negatively; and which can often do so to a considerable extent.

The socialising organisation

An organisation is a club. Colleagues are acquaintances or friends and work can be fun (not all the time perhaps, but it is a relevant objective), and this makes for problems as, for example, 'Good morning' turns into half the morning disappearing in chatter. It is an area where a time log may provide surprising information.

Now I am not suggesting that all social contact is forbidden, perish the thought. I like a chat as much as anyone; indeed, without some of this to foster relationships, an organisation would not only be duller, but a less effective place. There is an indefinable dividing line between the social chat and the business content, and curtailing anything we cannot definitely label 'business' will risk throwing the baby out with the bath water. On the other hand, you do need to keep things in proportion, curtail excesses and beware those moments when the danger is greatest – time will be really wasted. These include:

- **first thing in the morning, when greetings tend to turn into an in-depth analysis of the meal, date, TV or movie, sporting event or disaster of the previous evening;**
- **breaks, when the coffee comes round or people gather around the drinks machine;**
- **lunch, when even the process of discussing when to go, with whom, and where, assumes time-consuming proportions;**
- **the end of the day when everyone is getting tired and a chat is a welcome excuse to wind down early.**

There are places too where you are prone to get caught and conversation runs on. In some companies, Reception acts as a sort of plaza with people coming and going through it in different directions using their meeting as an excuse for a chat.

Because people's work patterns are different, moments when you have time for a chat may not suit others and vice versa. There needs to be mutual respect for people's time and concentration around an office, and everyone can play a part in fostering such a culture. For example, an earlier section advocated taking an occasional break to aid concentration. Do not, however, use these to break in on other people. Not only does this waste their time, but what you intended to be a two-minute pause may very easily turn into half an hour, two cups of coffee and, even if some of the conversation is useful, a major disruption of two people's schedules. So beware and be careful – there is no need to be stand-offish or to screen out useful conversations, but remember that this is a major factor eating away at productivity, and act accordingly.

Informal contact

You do need to see and talk to people. But, like so much else, how and when this is organised should be a conscious plan, one conditioned not least by the time that will be taken up. How do you approach this? This has become a technique in its own right, with its own abbreviation: MBWA. These initials stand for 'management by walking about', and it describes the need for management, perhaps especially senior management, to keep in touch at a direct and personal level with the other departments and people with whom they work. However good the management control systems in an organisation, there is no substitute for going and seeing and hearing for yourself what is going on, and what problems and opportunities exist.

Management can very often become protected and cloistered to the point that they have no genuine feel for how other parts of the organisation work. So not only is this sound advice, but it is a real aid to communication, and it can save time. At its most dramatic, one fact-finding walkabout can negate the need for several meetings and a report as the evidence of your own eyes and ears jumps you ahead in the decision-making process. Being in touch makes a real difference to your ability to operate, so the balance of time here – taken and saved – is likely to be productive. This is especially true if you can find ways of creating opportunities for this that serve more than one purpose.

I was given a good example of this recently when I was conducting a short course for a client company. The Managing Director both introduced the programme and came back to round things off at the end. This is, I believe, good practice, demonstrating a senior management commitment to what others are being asked to give up time for and generally supporting a training culture. At the end of the second day, drinks were available and at one moment as everyone was chatting, the Managing Director interrupted his discussion with one of his people to make notes – they had stumbled on a useful point and he noted it for later follow-up. This happened quite naturally as the chat mixed with more serious comment.

The point here was that the Managing Director, doubtless a busy man, consciously saw such a gathering as serving a double purpose: he was happy to support training, but more ready to do so if it provided an opportunity for some of the 'walking about' he felt was necessary anyway. He might have considered that giving just an introduction was not time well spent, but the addition of drinks and discussion – in fact taking longer – made it serve two purposes and become well worthwhile. Interesting.

Making a working lunch work

An army, it is said, marches on its stomach. In business too, we all have to pause now and then to refuel. What has this to do with time management? Consider the following phrases. First, 'business lunch'. For most people this conjures up something expensive, lengthy, and substantial. If you add in the time taken to get to such an event, then the total time involved is something to be considered very carefully. You need to think about whether to accept such invitations, or how often to do so. You may need to meet with the person concerned, but there may be other ways to achieve this. And you certainly need to think twice before you issue such invitations yourself. Again, the first question is whether a meeting is necessary, then whether it needs to be at lunch. Entertaining is, without a doubt, important. Some contacts (customers, suppliers and others) will not rate the business relationship so highly if you appear to take it for granted. Yet time is finite and you cannot do this every time you think of it. Each occasion should result from a considered decision and be worthwhile in its own right. Also consider simpler options. A meal out in a good restaurant or hotel may be too time-consuming for your contact (they are in all probability busy people too). What simpler options are there? Something in the office perhaps? It must be done well, but it does not need to be a gigantic meal or a time-consuming occasion to meet its objectives. You may well find this option is welcomed by some of your contacts.

Second, 'working lunch'. This is more often internal, and can be very simple – an urgent meeting scheduled for an appropriate hour with just coffee and sandwiches provided makes for productivity. Similarly, you may opt to go out for a simple snack with a colleague and do so to discuss a particular matter, often one that has previously escaped fitting into your schedule. All this is useful. Sometimes lunchtime needs to be something of a pause, but remember with around 220 working days in the year, an hour for lunch on each would add up to more than 25 working days! So, it is certainly an area to think about extremely carefully. A final, cautionary, note: watch what you drink at lunchtime. Alcohol may help relaxation but falling asleep at your desk later will certainly not improve productivity!

Consider a day out

Entertaining was just referred to, but it can take many forms and some of them are a good deal more time-consuming than lunch. Corporate entertaining (and I am not thinking so much of major group occasions such as sponsorship events) can include a wide variety of things from a night at the opera, to an evening in a karaoke bar; from a day at the races to a golf afternoon. Because they involve a very real cost, such things certainly need thinking about, but so too do the time considerations.

Take a golf outing as an example. Much business may really be conducted on the golf course, and I am not suggesting that such activity is never useful and should be entirely rejected, but its real merits do need assessing. It is not enough that you or your contact will enjoy whatever it is. Ask:

- **What will come of it?**
- **Will it genuinely move the relationship forward?**
- **Is there another way of achieving the same effect with less time expenditure?**
- **Can anyone else do it?**

All these questions need answering. Other factors come in here too. A golf outing on a Saturday morning, rather than on a weekday, may make good use of time, though too many may begin to eat into family time. If three contacts accompany you one day, then the time may be viewed differently from when there is only one.

Like so much discussed in this book, one more golf outing does not seem vastly significant, but it adds up. Two golf outings a month might use up the equivalent of a whole day, 5 per cent of your working time. You need to keep this in mind. Maybe a larger group of people once a month would work equally well. Whatever things of this nature form part of your working life, think about them not as an automatic part of the way things are –

unchangeable – but as time that needs to be utilised carefully just like any other. Then you can make the right decisions and know that time is not being wasted.

However and wherever contact occurs with other people, the nature of it will affect the duration of it. Being aware of this, especially in terms of the negative aspects of contact – and avoiding it – will save time.

No conflict – no wasted time

Now listen, pay attention. It is no good just sitting there lazily scanning the pages, you have to read this properly and... Not a good start. Sometimes an approach that is designed to get straight to the point and therefore not waste time has the reverse effect. It rubs people up the wrong way, and can produce misunderstanding, dissent or argument that in turn take time to resolve and the original intention goes out the window. Conflict is not, in fact, entirely bad. It can act as a catalyst to debate, it can help promote creativity and prompt a drive for the results necessary in business. But there is a real difference between this and allowing unnecessary conflict to disrupt the smooth running of things and your time being affected along with it. I am not suggesting here that the wrong decisions should be made for the sake of a quiet life, but in a number of areas conflict is to be avoided, for example:

- **In communications. It may be necessary to persuade rather than cajole, and time taken to do so successfully may pay dividends.**
- **Office politics (of which there is always some) can become intrusive and time-consuming; though ignoring it is dangerous in other ways, it must be kept in its place.**
- **Personalities can become more important than issues; commercial reason must dictate most of what directs an**

organisation, and untangling personality factors once
they have got out of hand takes time.
• Sectional interests also have to be watched.

Take this last as a simple example. Imagine that some internal
reorganisation is to change the physical layout of an office –
departments are going to move and, not surprisingly, sections are
worried about the priority they will be given and the new
conditions they will find. Yet, there are entirely practical issues
too. The design department needs good lighting, the customer
services department needs the most telephones, a department
with large amounts of stock in and out may need to be on the
ground floor, to take some very general ones. If consideration of
what will be decided, any discussions, meetings and everything
to do with the process, can be kept primarily on a practical basis
(there are other issues, of course); if conflict, in this case about
personal issues, can be avoided, the time taken to sort the whole
thing out will almost certainly be less. This has wide
implications, but shows the merit of always bearing in mind the
time element of everything you touch.

Circumstances that can create time-wasting because of
conflict can be momentary, something only demanding a
moment's thought to avoid, or more intractable, demanding real
effort and willpower to avoid when you are itching to draw up
battle lines. In either case, you should be on the lookout for such
circumstances and act to avoid their worst effects.

Next, a number of points are investigated predominantly for
those who, as managers, have other people reporting to them.
Many of the points made will have relevance to others on the
receiving end of such a relationship, or whose job is likely to
include such responsibilities at some time in the future.

The right people

The logical starting point is perhaps when such relationships are
created. Finding the right person for any job is a vital and

complex business, one too often underestimated. There are many considerations, certainly too many for this book to explore comprehensively, but of one thing you can be sure: recruiting the wrong people is going to waste time. It means:

- **performance being adversely affected;**
- **time taken up trying to correct the situation, and ultimately in discipline proceedings (and anything that touches on employment legislation is always time-consuming);**
- **replacing an inappropriate staff member;**
- **plugging gaps while all this is going on.**

Recruiting and selecting takes time, but it is time well spent (and a topic you may want to investigate separately). Maybe, also, you want to select people who are themselves good at managing time. This can certainly enhance the strength of any team you manage. Anyway, leaving the details of recruitment and selection aside, with the people in place you can consider what aspects of management are linked most closely to time management. One such is a key aspect of communication.

The need for clear instructions

There is an old saying that there is never time to do anything properly, but there must always be time to do it again. Nothing is more likely to end up being redone than not making it clear to people what they had to do in the first place. It has already been said here that communication is not easy, but the responsibility for getting it right is with the communicator – and that, if you are issuing instructions, is you. Similarly, if people do not really understand and fail to query it, perhaps because they are worried you will blame them, then that is also your fault because you should make it clear that in such circumstances it is the way they should proceed. So, instructions should be clear and people should be told:

- what needs to be done (and be given sufficient details);
- why it needs to be done (knowing the objectives may make the task clearer and will improve the motivation);
- how it should be done (methodology, etc);
- when it should be completed (and anything else about the timing).

Before leaving the point, ask if it is clear – get some feedback. Any shortcut of this sequence must be based on genuine knowledge or familiarity, not simply an assumption that all will be well. Good clear instructions save time; written guidelines do the same and for some jobs they are useful. This last is especially true of awkward or difficult jobs that are performed regularly but not often. One such job in my office is changing the printer's toner. It is not that complicated, but frankly it is difficult to do after the time gap usually involved without reference to a chart of diagrams that came with the machine and that shows clearly the sequence of actions needed to complete the task. The moment taken to get this chart out is tiny, much less than even minor pause for puzzlement about how to make the change without it, and it is all too easy with such a task to get in a real muddle and waste a considerable amount of time. Moral: all instructions, in whatever form, must be clear.

Don't do it – delegate

If a task simply has to be done, but you cannot get to it, then the best way to give yourself more time is to delegate it to someone else. This is eminently desirable and yet, for some, curiously difficult. What are the pros and cons?

First, the advantages. Consider these by asking yourself what sort of manager you want to work for yourself. You could probably list a great many qualities: someone who is fair, who listens, who is decisive, good at their job and so on – but I bet you would put someone who delegates high on the list. The opposite is a boss who hangs on to everything, does not involve you, is probably secretive and generally not the sort of person you would want to work for at all. So, if you delegate effectively, there are major advantages in other ways: motivation and the chance to tackle new things for one, as well as the time you will save.

Second, the difficulties. Delegating is a risk. Something may go wrong and what is more, as the manager, you may be blamed. So, despite the fact that going about it the right way will minimise the risk, there is temptation to hang on to things. This makes for problems in two ways. You have too much to do, and particularly too much at the more routine end, keeping you from giving things that are clear priorities the attention you know they deserve. And staff do not like it, so motivation – and productivity on the things they are doing – will also be adversely affected.

But there is another important and significant reason why delegation sometimes does not happen. This is fear – not that the other person will not be able to cope, but that they will cope too well, that they will improve the method, that they will do things more quickly, more thoroughly and better in some way than you. If you are honest, you may admit this is a real fear too. Certainly, it is a common one. Though it is precisely how innovation can occur. It is not a reason that should put you off delegating – the potential rewards are too great. The amount you can do if you delegate successfully is way beyond the improvement in productivity you can hope to achieve in any other way. So, it is a vital area. But what about something delegated that does go better? So much to the good, this is one of the key ways that progress is made in organisations as new people, new ways and new thinking are brought to bear on tasks. Without it, organisations would become stultified and unable to cope with change. And besides, as a manager you should be the reason they are able to make this happen. It is your selection, development, counselling and management that create and maintain a strong and effective team; and this is something for which you deserve credit.

Making delegation successful needs a considered and systematic approach to the process. What does successful delegation achieve? There are several key results. Delegation:

- **creates, for those to whom matters are delegated, opportunity for development and accelerated experience;**
- **builds morale (precisely because of the opportunity above) through the motivational effect of greater job satisfaction, and achievement long and short term in the job (and ultimately beyond it);**
- **has broader motivational effects around a team, as well as on the individual;**
- **for the delegator, concentrates time and effort on those aspects of their job that are key to the achievement of objectives;**
- **brings a more considered, or creative, approach to bear, uncluttered by matters that may distract or prevent a broad brush or longer-term perspective.**

You can probably think of specific advantages springing from these kinds of general effects in your own job. Yet, it can be curiously difficult to delegate, and some managers find it impossible. Just as you want to report to someone who delegates, so too will those who work for you. If the time gains to be made from delegation seem inadequate to make you do it, or do it as much as you should, maybe this will produce additional pause for thought. Despite the several and considerable advantages delegation can bring, it is not without its risks. This element of risk makes it difficult to accomplish, but several factors can help:

1. **Minimising the risks.** There is always the possibility that delegation will not work. After all, it passes on 'the right to be wrong' as it were, by putting someone else in the driving seat. So, if a misjudgement is made about the choice of what is to be delegated, to whom it is to be

delegated or how the process will be carried out, things may end up with mistakes being made, and time being wasted as a result. The net intention from all this must be to minimise the inherent risks, first by selecting tasks that are suitable for delegation. In most jobs there will be certain things that should sensibly be omitted. These include:

- matters key to overall results generation or control;
- staff discipline matters;
- certain contentious issues (eg staff grievances);
- confidential matters (though be sure they need to be confidential; protecting unnecessary secrets can be very time-wasting and often fruitless).

Then, in picking the best person to whom to delegate, you should ask questions such as:

- Have they undertaken similar tasks in the past?
- Do they have the necessary knowledge, experience and capability?
- Is it too much to cope with at once?
- Is prior training (however informal) necessary?
- Do they want to do more? (Or should they?)
- Will they be acceptable to others involved and will it be accepted also as a fair opportunity amongst peers?

Thereafter, perhaps the greatest guarantee of success is clear communication, and that means more widely than just with the person involved. Others may have to know what is going on and have to trust in the person's ability to do something. Messages may need to be passed up and down and across the line to ensure total clarity. Make sure there is nothing left out regarding authority, responsibility and that, above all, the individual concerned knows why the job is necessary and why they are doing it. And, as the result of any briefing, be confident that they are able to do it satisfactorily.

Any explanation needs to make clear whether what is being done is a one-off exercise, perhaps in an emergency, or ultimately a permanent addition to the existing set of responsibilities. Remember, delegation is more than simple work allocation and, as such, can have implications for such matters as job descriptions, salary and employment conditions. Assuming that delegation is well chosen and communicated, the next step is to keep in touch, at least initially, with how things are going.

2. **Monitoring progress.** Once something has been passed over, keeping in touch can easily be forgotten, and when done it can present certain problems. It must be done, in a word, carefully. If it is not, then it will smack of interference and may doom the whole process. The simplest way to monitor in an acceptable way is to build in any necessary checks at the time of the original briefing and handover. From the beginning, ask for interim reports at logical points. Do not simply arrive unannounced at someone's desk and ask to see the file (they may be at an awkward stage). Let them bring things to you, at prearranged moments. If they have been well briefed, know what is expected and to what standards, then they can deliver in a way that either duplicates past practice, or brings something new to the activity. Either may be appropriate in the short term, though, as nothing lasts for ever, new thinking is usually to be encouraged once the person has a real handle on the basics.

It may be necessary to let things proceed, to bite your tongue and resist taking the whole matter back during this stage as you see things proceeding in a way that may well differ, if only a little, from the way in which you would have done the job. The ultimate results make all this worthwhile, and not just in time terms but in terms of growth and development within the workplace. So far so good. If all goes well surely there is nothing more to be done? Wrong. The process must be evaluated.

3. **Evaluating how delegation has worked.** Once sufficient time has gone by and you can assess how things have gone, a number of questions should be asked. These can usefully include:

- Has the task been completed satisfactorily?
- Did it take an acceptable amount of time?
- Does it indicate the person concerned could do more?
- Are there other tasks that could be delegated along the same route?
- What has been the effect on others (eg are others wanting more responsibility)?
- Is there any documentation change necessary as a result?
- Has any new or revised methodology been created and are there implications arising from this (eg a change to standing instructions)?
- Overall, what has the effect been on productivity?

This last brings us to a key aspect of evaluation: what has the effect been on you? In other words: what have you done with the time saved? (This might make new work possible, or facilitate a greater focus on key or long-term issues.) There is little to be gained by delegating if you only end up submerged in more detail and having little or nothing of real substance to show for the change.

Similarly, should the process not be a success, questions should be asked about what went wrong and they too need to address both sides, asking not just what did someone do wrong or misunderstand, but also raising such questions as how thoroughly you in fact briefed that person. It is important to learn from the experience; testing what you delegate, to whom, and seeking the best way of handling the process is well worthwhile. If you develop good habits in this area, it can pay dividends over time.

At the end of the day, the effect on others is as important as the effect on you. People carry out with the greatest enthusiasm and care those things for which they have responsibility. In delegating you pass on the opportunity for additional responsibility (strictly speaking, responsibility can only be taken, you cannot force it on people) and you must also pass on with it the authority to act. As has been said, delegation fosters a good work ing relationship around a team of people. Not least, it produces challenge and, although there are risks, people will normally strive hard to make it work and the failure rate will thus be low. Certainly, the effect on productivity can be marked. But – there is always a but with anything of this sort – it is a process that needs care, determination and perhaps even sacrifice. Delegation is not just a way of getting rid of the things you regard as chores; among the matters most likely to benefit from delegation are almost certainly things you enjoy doing.

The potential rewards cannot be overrated, and the need to make delegation work is therefore strong. Theodore Roosevelt once said: 'The best executive is the one who has sense enough to pick good men to do what he wants done, and the self-restraint enough to keep from meddling with them while they do it.' Sound advice, and for the manager wanting to be a good time manager it is crucial. The two things go together. You cannot be as good at time management if you are a poor delegator. Get both right and you have a major part of the overall management process working for you. This is an area to think on:

- **Do you delegate?**
- **Do you delegate the right things and do it sufficiently often?**
- **How well does it work?**

While the principles reviewed here are important and it is something to be tackled on the right basis, an intention and commitment to making it work are perhaps most important. It may be worth more time to check it out. If you think there is more that you could delegate, review just what and just how you can action the process to get the very most from it in terms of your time and all the other advantages that can flow from it. Perhaps you should consider attending a course on delegating (or better still, send your assistant!).

Swap tasks to save time

Everyone has different skills and different things they get done most quickly and easily. Some of the things you find laborious, a colleague may think a small matter. As everyone is in this position, all you need to do is organise some exchanges. For example, in the sales office of one of my clients, two people did this very effectively. The department had to analyse, document and circulate sales results in various forms (to show sales progress, salespeople's targets and results by territory, etc). One person was very good at the analysis, sorting the untidy returns that came in from the sales team into an ordered set of information. The other was good at presenting the information in graphic form – using software they knew backwards and others did not.

In the official work allocation, they had both been given the complete job to do for different product sales results. In effect, they swapped and all the analysis was done by one, while all the graphic representation was done by the other. The entire job was completed more easily and faster and there was more time to apply to other tasks, primarily dealing with customers, which made up their responsibilities. They felt it was a fair swap in time terms and all worked well.

This is something that can be done in all sorts of ways around groups of people working together, or even in different departments. There is only one snag to watch out for and that is any developmental role that is part of a job having been allocated to someone in the first place. If a manager expects you to become familiar with a task and build up some sort of expertise in it, then you are not likely to do that by letting someone else do the work. That apart, it works well as an idea and you may want to be on the lookout for suitable swap situations that will help you. They must turn out to be fairly balanced, of course – if one party ends up with far more work than the other, then the arrangement will falter, as someone will end up unhappy. More complex swaps, for example two smaller tasks for one larger one, may achieve a suitable balance. Choose well and you may evolve a number of such arrangements all around the organisation, all saving you time. As long as the network does not become too complicated (it must continue to work when you are away for a while, and deadlines must be compatible) then it is one more useful way of saving time on a regular basis.

Develop your people

It was clear earlier, I hope, that delegation is one of the greatest opportunities for managers to create more time for themselves.

There is one potential snag, however, simply that the people to whom you delegate must have the necessary skill and aptitude to take on delegated tasks and make a good job of them. What their skill level actually is depends largely on you. You recruit and select them, and one of your responsibilities is helping them to develop.

Training and development is one of those things that most people agree is a 'good thing', yet it is also something that is all too easy to miss out when you are busy. Here is an additional reason to make sure that it does not get overlooked: help your people develop and they will help you do your job, because not only will the team perform better, but you will be able to delegate more to them.

As a responsible manager, you should have an individual development plan for every single person who reports to you. This will stem in part from their annual appraisal meeting and evaluation, and can usefully include: things that you will do, for example by personal counselling; things they will do, such as private study and experiment and practice; and things that, as it were, the organisation will do for them, such as sending them on a course or providing other training resources for them to use.

The criteria that decide what development is necessary will arise from an analysis of a person's job, defining what is necessary to do it, then determining whether the person matches up to this or whether there is a skills gap that must be closed by training. In addition, the manager has to look ahead, asking how the job will be different in future because such changes may widen the training gap. Topics for training range wide (from the technical to personal skills), but they should include a link with your job as manager and anticipate possible delegation opportunities.

What tasks must you cope with during the next year and what other things might you shed to make room for the new things you have to tackle? The obvious choices for matters to delegate are those that staff can already do competently. But it may well be worth looking more broadly at what possibilities there are if some development is done first.

This can be a classic case of a positive balance: time investment is necessary, but the pay-off can often be well worthwhile. It is a pity if the longer-term nature of this process makes it less likely to be taken advantage of because, not only will you save time, but it will also lead to the other advantages of delegation: personal motivation and stimulation to the process of running the organisation.

Simply the most time-saving phrase in the language

There is a scene that is played out in offices all over the world and that must waste untold hours every single day. Imagine a manager is busy in his or her office when a head comes round the door and a member of staff comes in. 'What is it?' the manager asks. And the reply is something like: 'I am not sure how to handle such-and-such and wondered if you would just check it with me.' The manager thinks for a second. He or she is busy – in the middle of a job and not wanting to lose concentration – but has already been interrupted. So, his or her first thought is to minimise the interruption and get back to work fast. If the matter allows, the manager spends a minute or two explaining what to do and then tells the other person to let them get on, and the brief impromptu meeting ends. This may be done kindly or abruptly, the effect is much the same, and the one manager may play out the scene many times in a day.

But suppose the same manager is away from the office for a couple of days. In his or her absence, staff face similar situations. If the manager were in, they would go and ask. In the manager's absence, they simply get on with the job. When the manager returns what does he or she find? A chain of disasters? A plethora of wrong decisions and misjudged actions? Rarely. The things the manager would have checked if he or she had been there have been actioned, and not only is no harm done, everything has probably gone perfectly well.

Think about it. I suspect this picture will ring bells with many, if not most, managers. Why does it happen? It is a classic case of thinking that it is quicker to do things for people, most often by providing the answer or making a decision. They take action, and life goes on. I believe this is wrong. You have to take a longer-term view, and this is where the most time-saving phrase in the language comes in.

Next time you are interrupted in the way I have described, try responding by saying: 'What do you think you should do?' They may not know, but you can press the point, prompt them to make some suggestions, and when they do, then ask which solution they think is best. This takes a few minutes, certainly longer than the earlier response, but if they are coping when you are not there to ask, then you will find that when you prompt them they most often come up with a good answer (in business there is rarely any one right way). Then you can say something like: 'That's fine', and away they go to carry on, leaving you to get back to your own work.

Now this is not just a better way of dealing with this situation. It is doing something else of very real value: it is teaching them not to interrupt, but rather to have the confidence to think it through for themselves. You have to be insistent about this. It will not work if you make them think it through only when you have more time, and still provide a quick answer when you are busy. Every time – every single time – someone comes through the door with a question about something with which you believe they should be able to deal unaided, you say: 'What do you think you should do?' It must become a catchphrase. And as this practice continues, the message will get home to them, so that if they even start to think of asking you they can hear your likely response in their mind.

If you do this, you will find such questions coming less and less often. You will find that if they do ask, they move straight to the second stage, and come in with two or three thought-out options just wanting you to say which is best. Resist; ask them. The message will stick and, surprise, surprise, you will find you are saving time. What is more, your people will almost certainly get to like it more also, especially if you comment favourably on how well they are doing on the decisions they are making unaided.

This is one of the best-tested and useful time savers around – the most time-saving phrase in the language – and all it needs is some persistence and determination. Early on, you may think it is taking too much time, but the investment formula will surely pay off. There are considerable amounts of time to be saved here, linked in fact to the number of people who report to you. Do not be faint-hearted about this, it is very easy to break your resolve in a busy moment and send someone on this way with an instant dictated solution. Exceptions to your consistency will just make the lesson take longer to get over. But this idea really does work in the longer term. Not to operate this way does your people a disservice and allows you to miss out on one of the best time savers managers can find.

Do not hover

However work has been passed on, whether it is simple work allocation or a job that has been delegated, managers have to give members of their team space to complete the tasks they are working on. There is a temptation, perhaps particularly when a job is first delegated and you worry whether it will be done right, not only to check up but to do so on an ad hoc basis. Because this is off-putting to those who may be at some mid-point on a job – a point at which things are not finished and look that way – it can actually end up delaying things and perhaps give you a false impression of their capabilities. These checks take time and may set back the way things are going rather than help. Certainly, they do nothing for motivation.

Do not hover. If something needs checking, and it may well do, then such checks should be discussed and agreed at the start of the work. Then the people concerned know what to expect. They can plan for any checks at particular moments and such checks will, as a result, be more likely to be constructive – or indeed unnecessary as those concerned will work to make sure that when the monitoring process arrives all is on schedule.

If you work to make such checks an agreed part of the plan, if you make them constructive, then you will not have to spend very much time on them at all. The team working well, with minimal supervision, is a great asset to any manager wanting to conserve his or her own time.

Motivate your people

Motivation is a powerful force. By acting on people's knowledge and ability, it can improve performance, efficiency and productivity – and save time. But, like so much else in management, this does not just happen. Unless you work at it, and that means some time will be taken up, you will not get the best from people, and that means some time will be wasted. Again, the equation of time here makes sense; the net effect should be a saving.

Motivation has been described as a climate and this is not a bad analogy. Just like the temperature in a room, many different things can affect people's motivation, and the effect can be for good or ill. There is sadly no magic formula for guaranteeing that motivation will be, and will stay, high. You have to look at the motivational implications of things such as the administration and systems with which people work, the way they relate to colleagues and to you as supervisor, and their feeling of security in the sense of knowing what they have to do and being part of a good team. All these can pull motivation down if they are organised badly or unsympathetically.

Whether it is time given to organising an incentive scheme or just saying 'Well done', it is time well spent. The details are beyond our brief here (and are looked at in detail in *How to Motivate People*), suffice it to say that a poorly motivated person will always take more time to manage than someone well motivated.

Provide specific time management help for staff

People who work together in an office can be infected by the prevailing practices and habits. In an office where some people habitually arrive late in the morning and nothing is said, more people will tend to follow suit and the situation will spread and get worse. This is a negative point, but here I am more concerned with the positive. If you want time management to be an issue that people care about, think about and work at, then you must take the initiative and lead by example. Several practices may be useful here, for example:

- **Set up standard systems. It is not too dictatorial to set up, and insist on, certain systems that you feel will help everyone's time utilisation; for example, the same priority codes used around the office, the same basis for completing diaries (or even the same diary or time** system), an insistence on tidy desks – you can probably think of more.

- Use standard reporting procedures. Here again a standard helps; such things as memo style, when, where and how meetings are scheduled, notice boards, all can help create a climate of efficiency if they are well organised.
- Explain. If you tell people why you do certain things, work in certain ways and why you expect them to do likewise then it is more likely that, seeing good and personally useful reason, they will comply (you can go further and organise training for them).

With practice, habits follow and then the time saving around and amongst a group of people accumulates. So, be a public advocate for the virtues of time management, say you believe in it, say you practise it, and do not just expect your team to follow suit – make it easy for them by introducing them to the systems and laying down a few rules to make it all stick. If you help them in these kinds of ways, it will help you too.

Make and keep some firm rules

The days of dictatorial management have, by and large, long gone. Management in today's environment necessarily involves consultation. It makes sense. People will go along much more wholeheartedly with things – policies, practices, whatever – if they feel they have played some part in their origination. At its most powerful, this creates what is nowadays called ownership and is a force for commitment and getting results. But there are limits. Just because consultation is a good thing, it does not mean that you have to consult, interminably, over everything. To balance the time this takes, you need other areas where, while the policy is sensibly constituted, there is no debate and no time wasted on it. An example will perhaps help make this clear – see the text opposite.

Time-saving rules – a case study

Every office has administration and form-filling that needs to be done. It seems a chore but the information is no doubt useful in some way or should be! (Why else is it being obtained?) Sometimes in an office, this form-filling is resisted. People know it is useful, but they also see other things as more important. They probably are, but that does not mean that the forms should never get filled in; besides, the individual contributions may, when collated, provide key information. So, what happens? People delay, forms come in late or incomplete and have to be returned and redone, sometimes more than once.

In one office, this was the case with the kind of control forms that field salespeople must complete to keep sales figures and the customer database updated. Salespeople are notoriously bad at administration and forms would regularly appear late, maybe half – and a different half – needing to be chased each month. The sales manager's secretary wasted time doing the chasing, and the sales manager had to keep explaining to his boss why the collated statistics were not available, as even one outstanding meant that the collation could not take place. It was generally messy and unsatisfactory and something had to be done to sharpen things up.

The sales manager thought about it. First, he checked that the system was the minimum necessary, and that the forms were straightforward to complete. He thought of various checks, but reckoned each could well waste still more time. Finally, he hit on the following scheme: he revised the instruction about the system so that no one was to be reimbursed their monthly expenses until all their forms were received and were passed as clear, legible and complete. Eureka! Overnight the behaviour was changed and all the forms arrived on time. What is more the effect lasted and I now know a number of companies who use the exact same incentive. The scheme was seen as reasonable and necessary, the new announcement of it was well put and the results spoke for themselves.

The most important thing happening here was that there was a group agreement that certain things simply had to go right without a lot of time being spent to achieve them. The incentive is neat, but there might be numerous things a manager could do in such circumstances to add a bit of an edge to the rule.

The case study makes a good example, but the important thing is that there should be certain areas where you operate in this sort of way. There is a firm rule, possibly a sanction, and it is clearly understood that there will be no exceptions, no excuses and no time wasted. If something does go wrong having set up things on this basis, then you have to descend from a great height and read the riot act – and do so consistently.

Such rules provide major time saving. Have a think about the things that go on in your office and amongst your people. You may well have some candidate systems or procedures that are due this sort of treatment. If so, start working on them soon. It is another area that can, in itself, not only save time, but also help to position attitudes and develop the right habits.

Meetings – danger or opportunity?

It is said that the ideal meeting consists of two people – with one absent! And another saying (and the title of a training film) refers to meetings, bloody meetings. There is truth in both, yet meetings are an important part of organisational communication, consultation and debate. We need them. Or, certainly, we need some of them, but we must get the most from them, and we do not need too many, or those that are longer than necessary or, above all, those that are unconstructive. So, this is an important topic to relate to time management, and certainly a major potential cause of time waste. Let us be positive and consider what meetings can do in that light.

Whatever the meeting, large or small, formal or informal, long or short, if it is actively planned, considered and conducted to make it go well, then it can be made to work. Meetings have various purposes: to inform, analyse and solve problems, discuss and exchange views, inspire and motivate, counsel and reconcile conflict, obtain opinion and feedback, persuade, train and develop, reinforce the status quo, impress and progress projects in a variety of ways.

You can no doubt expand the list. The key purpose is surely most often to prompt change (there is no point in having a meeting if everything remains the same), and this means making decisions. So any meeting has to be constructive. It must put people in a position where good decisions can prompt appropriate action.

Note also that good meetings are not just useful, they can also stimulate discussion and action that would never occur unless a particular group got together. What makes for a good meeting?

Setting up meetings

If a meeting is to be truly successful, then ensuring its success cannot begin only as the meeting starts – the 'I think we're all here, what shall we deal with first?' school of meeting organisation. Making it work starts before the meeting, sometimes some time before. First, ask some basic questions, for example:

- Is a meeting really necessary?
- Should it be a regular meeting? (Think very carefully about this one – once a meeting is designated as the weekly, monthly or whatever, it can become a routine that is difficult to break and as such can be an especially easy way to waste time.)
- Who should attend? (And who should not?)

If you are clear in these respects then you can proceed. Some key points to bear in mind include:

- *Setting an agenda.* This is very important; no meeting will go as well if you simply make up the content as you get under way (notify the agenda in advance and give good notice of contributions required from others).
- *Timing.* Set a start time *and* a finishing time, then you can judge the way it is to be conducted alongside the duration and even put some rough timings to individual items to be dealt with. Respect the timing too: start on time and try to stick with the duration planned.
- *Objective.* Always set a clear objective so that you can say why a meeting is being held (and the reason should never be – *because it is a month since the last one!*).
- *Prepare yourself.* Read all necessary papers, check all necessary details and think about how you will handle both your own contribution and the stimulation, and control, of others.
- *Insist others prepare also.* This may mean instilling habits (eg pausing to go through something that should have been studied before the meeting only shows that reading beforehand is not really necessary).
- *People.* Who should be there (or not) and what roles individuals should have.
- *Environment.* A meeting will go much more smoothly if people attending are comfortable and uninterrupted (so organise switching the coffee pot on and the phones off before you start).

Then, at the appointed hour, someone must take charge and make the meeting go well.

Leading a meeting

Even a simple meeting needs someone in the chair. That does *not* imply that whoever it is must be the most senior person present, do most of the talking or even lead the talking, or that they need to be formally called 'chairperson' – but someone must *direct* the meeting. An effective chairperson can ensure a well-directed meeting and in turn means:

- **The meeting will better focus on its objectives.**
- **Discussion can be kept more constructive.**
- **A thorough review can be assured before ad hoc decisions are taken.**
- **All sides of the argument or case can be reflected and balanced.**
- **Proceedings can be kept businesslike and less argumentative (even when dealing with contentious issues).**

Thus, all the results of effective chairing are positive, and all allow a meeting to be succinct. To summarise, a good chairperson will lead the meeting, handle the discussion and act to see objectives are met, promptly, efficiently and effectively and without wasting time.

Some of what must be done is simple. Much is common sense; the whole of the role is important. Two simple but key rules that any chairperson must stick to (and which all present should respect) are: only one person may talk at a time and the chairperson decides who (when necessary).

Already all this begins to highlight the qualities of the person who will make a good 'chair'. It is always a vital role. They must command respect, ensure order and ensure that the discussion moves purposefully towards its objectives. They must listen, summarise and, on occasion, pour oil on troubled waters. Effectively they are 'in charge', though this needs to be diplomatically achieved. Finally, consider two other important factors.

Getting off to a good start

The best meetings start well, continue well and end well. The chairperson should start the meeting in a way that:

- **is positive;**
- **makes its purpose (and procedure) clear and seen to be businesslike;**
- **establishes the chairperson's authority and right to be in charge;**
- **creates the right atmosphere (whether to prompt creative thinking or, say, detailed analysis of figures);**
- **generates interest and enthusiasm for the topics (yes, even for a tedious regular review).**

It usually helps if the chairperson involves others early on, rather than beginning with a lengthy monologue. This indicates a final point.

Prompting discussion

Of course, sometimes *prompting* contributions is the least of the problems, but you want contributions from everyone (or why are they there?). So, to ensure you get adequate and representative discussion and that subsequent decisions are made on all the appropriate facts you may need to prompt discussion.

Watch for specific reasons for silent participants. For example: they may fear rejection or pressure of other, more senior or more powerful, people, be unprepared, have an incomplete understanding of what has gone before or, indeed, may simply need encouragement. A good chairperson will ask for views and prompt open, considered comments.

Remember tone or manner can easily skew comments. For in stance, someone senior is unlikely to encourage creative suggestions by fielding their own thoughts first: 'It is only a suggestion, but do bear in mind who's making it.' So, do not lead.

Questions make the best prompt: deployed to ensure you have the measure of different individuals, drawing in, say, the more reticent and acting to keep the overbearing or less businesslike in check. Questions must be unambiguous. *Open questions* that cannot be answered 'yes' or 'no', questions starting what, why, where, when, how and similar or phrased: 'Tell me about...' or 'What do you think about...?' work best. They get people talking rather than encouraging a monosyllabic reply that adds little. *Closed questions* are better when you want a short, specific response. Right?

In many organisations, meetings are unproductive or unconstructive not because how they are undertaken is ill-considered, but because making them successful is hardly considered at all. There is a real opportunity here (worth convening a meeting to discuss?). Time spent making sure that meetings do not waste time is time well spent. And careful planning, and attention to necessary detail, will make sure meetings go well and that is even more important. People are major time wasters; but they are also allies in creating productivity.

8

Final words

> Next week there can't be any crisis. My
> schedule is already full.
>
> *Henry Kissinger*

Making time management work is important to everyone. At
worst, the alternative is a life of permanent muddle, pressure and
frustration – not to mention the fact of actually achieving less
than you would want or believe possible. So, there are
considerable advantages to getting to grips with the process. To
recap: principally, effective management of your time will allow
you to:

- achieve greater productivity, efficiency and
  effectiveness;
- give more focus to your efforts and make any particular
  way of working, for example creativity, easier;
- be more likely to achieve your various objectives;
- be more likely to be able to develop the job long term;
- get more satisfaction and enjoyment from what you
  do;

- **find that home and family and job responsibilities fit better together.**

These benefits incorporate many things, from fewer missed deadlines to more time for key projects and better relationships with the people working with or for you in the organisation. Further, because time management affects results and efficiency so directly, it can have a direct bearing on your career progress.

So, there certainly seem to be more than sufficient reasons to make it work for you. Some of the ideas that help seem very obvious and when you take them up they quickly fit in, become habits and work well without great effort. Other aspects of the process are, as we have seen, inevitably harder. At the end of the day, is time management really something to bother about or is it just another management panacea, actually only taking up time that could be better spent simply getting on and doing the job? I firmly believe that it is not just worthwhile, but essential. I hope this book has demonstrated that the time it takes to become better organised need not be prohibitive, indeed that, as good habits develop, the techniques, tricks and, most important, the attitudes adopted clearly pay dividends.

What makes it all work is not simply having an understanding of the principles and enough ideas, but the discipline and ultimately the habit to make it stick as an overall way of working.

The results stemming from it have been stated. Even so, is the net effect worthwhile? I believe the answer is certainly yes. It is one business technique that not only affects the organisation through the individual's job and the results it generates, but also affects the individual – your job satisfaction, state of mind and general well-being. Becoming a better time manager may take a commitment, and needs working at, but, as the saying has it, 'There is no such thing as a free lunch.' Most worthwhile things do need some investment of time and effort. This is no exception. It is no exaggeration to say that good time management can change your life quickly for the better and, if you foster the habits involved, forever (or, more realistically, for the remainder of your career).

Eternity is a terrible thought. I mean, where is it going to end?

Tom Stoppard

Appendix 1: Time management to the rescue

> Throwing an eleven foot rope to someone drowning twenty feet from the river bank is more than meeting them halfway.
>
> *Lenny Bruce*

Recession, depression, whatever you may call it, as I write this in early 2009 we are certainly going through tough times and it seems worth making a link between this here. Indeed any difficult or pressurised period has a strong link with time management. Consider the nature of tough times first.

Be sure of one thing – waiting for things to get back to normal is just not an option. To manage – even survive - in tough times demands action; and you must not panic – keeping a cool head is vital.

But, while action may need to be prompt (or things could get worse) action must also be well considered. So, despite the fact that day-to-day activity is doubtless extra hectic, you must find time to:

- **Review possible action; and such a review must be systematic, wide ranging and creative.**

- Consider all parts of the business and include all possibilities and possibly radical – or distasteful – action in the decision making.
- Ensure such a review examines both current practice – to ensure it remains sensible in the new circumstances - and possible new solutions too.

Overall the options are not so many:

- Costs may need to be cut (though care must be taken that this does not make matters worse, for example wholesale cutting of marketing costs may simply reduce sales still further).
- Customers, revenue and profitability must be protected and this may mean acting to obtain a larger share of a reducing market. This latter means that the effectiveness of all activity must be maximised: for example sales and marketing activity must be well targeted and well executed.
- Reorganisation (for instance of finances, personnel and marketing processes).
- Looking for new, revised and creative ways of doing things in every aspect of the business.

Where action such as reducing staff is necessary, it is better taken promptly but with as much compassion as possible (you may want to rehire people). The last thing you want is to be struggling to work in difficult markets with a de-motivated workforce while management rushes around in panic. You may be unable to stop the recession in its tracks, but you can surely mitigate its effect by responding in a considered, systematic way that reflects the new realities. Overall, everything done must:

- be the result of deploying sufficient time for a constructive review – on a regular basis;
- maintain a customer focus; customers remain more important than anything else;

- maintain continuity (especially of marketing activity);
- allocate clear personal responsibility.

At the end of the day, as we finally emerge from recession (as ultimately we must), those who come through in best order will have:

- thought ahead and focused on the broad picture;
- have had a clear plan and clear goals throughout – goals that are challenging, well defined, desirable and realistic;
- believed they can make a difference and instilled this belief in their people;
- deployed appropriate knowledge and skills both themselves and from their team to ensure that action was always well executed.

But there's a problem...

The problem is that in any period of difficulty, recession or otherwise, the need for emergency, ad hoc and what is often called fire-fighting action escalates. The comments above may sound like so much common sense, but they demand time of people throughout the organisation. Consideration and a cool head are necessary just when people's every instinct is crying out for them to drop everything and rush off and sort out some immediate problem right now.

Time management becomes vital in such circumstances. If the only criterion in selecting what to do next becomes the perceived urgency, then it can become effectively impossible to find time for the review, consultation and careful consideration that should be deployed to seek action and solutions that may, if not cure the difficulties, at least reduce the damage done. It is easy to find yourself in circumstances where you look back and find yourself saying something that starts with the words 'If only ...'. You recognise that action could have been taken, should have been taken, and know – with that 20/20 hindsight that comes so easily to us all – that if it had been taken some aspect of the difficulty could have been reduced or avoided.

Recognising this possibility ahead of times is the first step to making sure that good time management practice can help in a crisis. In fact:

- **Those who have good time management habits as part of their normal practice are likely to cope best; and this applies to whole teams as well as individuals.**
- **Those who recognise and avoid the temptation of being diverted into fire-fighting and keep that under control (some things are urgent and must be addressed at once) and take time to ensure time is available to consider and respond to adverse conditions are also likely to survive tough times better.**

Most people would agree that often in a busy life the most difficult kind of time to find is time to think. Yet there are many circumstances where this is essential. It assists creativity and it assists in times of difficulty, when creativity may be the only way to some sort of solution. So often, as has been said here, the tendency is to rush into action, some action, any action, and consideration goes out the window. And the first thing jumped at may not be best or even appropriate; as H L Menkin said, 'There is always a well known solution to every human problem: neat, plausible... and wrong'.

So, as we draw towards the end, let me say this: a mere appearance of time management will not maximise your performance, much less get you out of trouble. Paying lip service to it will never be the same as a real commitment.

The following classic tale makes a sobering point:

A medieval King is crossing the forest with his entourage on a hunting trip. On a series of trees they see a painted target and in the exact centre of each there is an arrow. 'What incredible accuracy' says the King 'We must find the archer'.

Further on they catch up with a small boy carrying a bow and arrow.

He is frightened at being stopped by the King's party, but admits that he fired the arrows. 'You did shoot the arrows, didn't you?' queried the King. 'You didn't just stick them into the targets by hand?' The boy replies 'Your majesty, I swear I shot all the arrows from a hundred paces'. 'Incredible', said the King. 'You must accept a job at the palace, I must have an archer of such brilliance near me. But tell me, you are so young, how do you achieve such accuracy?'

The boy looked sheepish. 'Well,' he said, 'first I step out a hundred paces, then I fire the arrow into the tree... and then I walk back and paint the target on the tree'.

Similarly just having a clever time management diary system or whatever will do you no good without the philosophy and techniques to take matters forward. It is using the principles and adopting matching working habits that allow you to focus on key issues that make a difference to performance. The lessons in this book can make a difference every day; they can certainly make a difference in difficult times – and when is that needed more? So, an immediate response to difficult times should be to refocus on your time management and make it help, not to throw all your habits and good practice out the window and resort primarily to fire-fighting

Note: if you are in difficult times when you read this, check out the book *Tough Tactics for Tough Times* by Patrick Forsyth and Frances Kay (Kogan Page).

Appendix 2: Time management format examples

The text in this book has conveyed the philosophy of time management, the attitudes and convictions that it demands, and how-to practical elements. To augment the last two points, it is often useful to use various formats to prompt and formalise your organisation.

Earlier I advised caution in adopting proprietary systems: trying to shoehorn yourself into what is actually someone else's system and finding a mismatch. But there is a profusion of more flexible systems, Filofax, referred to previously, being probably the best known. Putting together a number of formats chosen (maybe after some experiment) because they suit *you* is most likely to give you something useful – and if you develop a good system you are more likely to develop good habits around it. Thus, in turn, you will continue to use the system in place and benefit from it on a daily basis.

Whatever you do, and however you organise it (in everything from a traditional loose-leaf binder to a computer or PDA screen) such formats can bring discipline to your intentions and help you get a grip on your time and avoid the mess of reality. At this stage, having read the book and perhaps having selected and organised some mechanisms to assist you, it is up to you. It is your time. Take the initiative, manage it effectively and it is you who will reap the benefit – in your job and in your career. The forms that follow in Figures A1 to A5 give you an idea of the purpose, style and possibilities of the formats that can help you get and stay organised:

A1. **Diary.** Surely everyone needs this, but there are choices to be made particularly regarding how much time – a day, a week or whatever – appears on a page. The example shows one week to a view page-design, with room for both appointments and tasks (symbols save space too, whether they are part of a standard form or ones you invent and use).

A2. **Year planner.** In conjunction with a diary this allows the relationship between widely spaced events to be seen at a glance, enabling matters that need planning to be easily considered.

A3. **Day planner.** A form that, alongside a diary, allows you to plan and work with the daily round of activities, events and tasks (again, symbols can assist and save space).

A4. **Action sheet.** A more freestyle form providing a flexible way to prompt, prioritise and record actions.

A5. **Meeting planner.** A form to allow you to plan effective meetings and avoid some of the many dangers meetings present and which were itemised earlier in the text.

Of course, many more forms can be used or originated: expenses, contact records (and for specific categories such as customers), analysis sheets, planning for specific tasks and more. The use of such things is inherently flexible and gives a practical edge to time management intentions. Filofax have a saying: plan it, do it and record it. Succinctly put – it is good advice.

January Janvier Januar Enero Gennaio   Week 1

Monday *3*	Tuesday *4*	Wednesday *5*
Lundi **UK**	Mardi **SC**	Mercredi
Montag	Dienstag	Mittwoch
Lunes	Martes	Miércoles
Lunedì	Martedì	Mercoledì
3-362	4-361	5-360
8	8	8
9	9	9
10	10	10
11	11	11
12	12	12
13	13	13
14	14	14
15	15	15
16	16	16
17	17	17
18	18	18
19	19	19
20	20	20
☎	☎	☎
✍	✍	✍

Figure A1

	Mon	Tue	Wed	Thu	Fri	Sat	Sun	Mon	Tue	Wed	Thu	Fr
Jan						1	2	3 **1**	4	5	6	7
Feb		1	2	3	4	5	6	7 **6**	8	9	10	11
Mar		1	2	3	4	5	6	7 **10**	8	9	10	11
Apr				1	2	3		4 **14**	5	6	7	8
May							1	2 **18**	3	4	5	6
Jun			1	2	3	4	5	6 **23**	7	8	9	10
Jul				1	2	3		4 **27**	5	6	7	8
Aug	1 **31**	2	3	4	5	6	7	8 **32**	9	10	11	12
Sep				1	2	3	4	5 **36**	6	7	8	9
Oct				1	2	3		3 **40**	4	5	6	7
Nov		1	2	3	4	5	6	7 **45**	8	9	10	11
Dec			1	2	3	4		5 **49**	6	7	8	9

JANUARY

WK	M	T	W	T	F	S	S
52						1	2
1	3	4	5	6	7	8	9
2	10	11	12	13	14	15	16
3	17	18	19	20	21	22	23
4	24	25	26	27	28	29	30
5	31						

FEBRUARY

WK	M	T	W	T	F	S	S
5		1	2	3	4	5	6
6	7	8	9	10	11	12	13
7	14	15	16	17	18	19	20
8	21	22	23	24	25	26	27
9	28						

MARCH

WK	M	T	W	T	F	S	S
9		1	2	3	4	5	6
10	7	8	9	10	11	12	13
11	14	15	16	17	18	19	20
12	21	22	23	24	25	26	27
13	28	29	30	31			

APRIL

WK	M	T	W	T	F	S	S
13					1	2	3
14	4	5	6	7	8	9	10
15	11	12	13	14	15	16	17
16	18	19	20	21	22	23	24
17	25	26	27	28	29	30	

Figure A2

		⧗	✉	☎	Action	✓
8						
9						
10						
11						
12						
1						
2						
3						
4						
5						
6						
7						
8						

Figure A3

	Action		
	☎	✍	✓

Figure A4

		✓
1		
2		
3		
4		
5		
6		
7		
8		
9		
10		

Figure A5

Creating Success series

The above titles are available from all good bookshops.
For further information on these and other Kogan Page titles, or
to order online, visit the Kogan Page website at
www.koganpage.com